AN INSIDER'S MANUAL TO LAUNCHING YOUR ACTING CAREER

THE ACTOR'S GUIDE

AN INSIDER'S MANUAL TO LAUNCHING YOUR ACTING CAREER

THE ACTOR'S GUIDE

SARAH VALENTINE

The Actor's Guide
An Insider's Manual to Launching Your Acting Career

© 2024 by Sarah Valentine. All rights reserved.

A catalogue record for this book is available from the National Library of New Zealand

ISBN: 978-0-473-69989-5

Published 2024 by Sarah Valentine

The moral rights of the author have been asserted

Book cover design: Lori Jackson
Cover photo: Andi Crown
Cover photo edit: Michelle Lancaster @lanefotograf
Interior design and formatting by: E.M. Tippetts Book Designs

CONTENTS

WELCOME

Hi, I'm Sarah; welcome to my book.

I have spent the last 30 years working behind and in front of the camera. I have worked as a casting director, an actors agent, an actor, an accent coach, and in many more on and off set positions. People often ask me how I ended up in all these different roles and what they could do to gain similar experience. I decided the best thing for me to do was to gather up all the knowledge and experience I have gleaned over my decades in the acting industry, and put it into a guide for other actors to use.

I've known for as long as I can remember that I wanted to act. I got my first paid gig in my 20's and I'm still out there going to auditions and giving it my best shot. In my experience, there is nothing easy about being an actor. There are highs and there are lows. There are good days and there are bad days, but when you get that audition or that role, there is no better feeling.

The purpose of this book is to help you to get started and also to keep you moving if you're feeling stuck. It can sometimes feel like your fate is not in your own hands as an actor, but trust me, there is plenty you can do to take control of your own progression. Don't sit around waiting to be discovered. Get out there and be the discoverer of all the things you never knew you could do.

And if you learn nothing else from reading this book, please remember this:
The only person that's going to get you to where you want to go is you, so let's get going!

XOXO Sarah

INTRODUCTION

This book is split into three acts plus an encore. We begin in Act One; this is where you'll get advice on how to best prepare yourself for the journey ahead and the small steps you can make now before taking bigger ones.

In Act Two, we'll look at your study options which include film and TV production, drama schools and online options. What skills can you learn to bolster your confidence and further propel you into the world of acting?

In Act Three, we look at the working life of actors. From joining unions to signing contracts, the buzz of preproduction and rehearsals. What you can expect as an actor, and what you may experience. Please note that this section of the book covers some sensitive topics such as sexual harassment and assault.

Lastly, the Encore. This covers more personal topics, including managing your mental health, your relationships, and the experiences of women in the industry. As a bonus, I've added in an interview I completed with Oscar winning actress Holly Hunter, who I worked with on the *Top of the Lake* TV series. I hope you enjoy reading about her acting and career insights. She is so dear to me, and her wealth of experience is such a bonus to this book.

Working on *Top of the Lake* with Holly Hunter, Pete Mullan and Elizabeth Moss was my career highlight, and it's where I got to work with director Jane Campion. Throughout this book, I will refer to my experiences on this show a lot, because working on Jane's set was simply one of the best and most transformative experiences of my acting career.

As you journey through each act in this book, you'll essentially learn all I know about the industry and get the inside scoop. You might read this book from start to finish, or you may choose specific chapters that you need to read now. Read what piques your interest; the other chapters might become more important later on as your career progresses. Remember, this book covers things you COULD do to help yourself along. There is no expectation that you would do everything suggested all at once. Just work on your skills bit by bit. It also covers things you MIGHT experience as an actor, but you may not. This is not an instruction manual; it is a guide, a prompt, a push and a prod from me to you.

Act One begins with the assumption that you know you want to act and have started your acting journey, no matter how big or small. Now is the time to make a more concerted effort to launch your career. This is when you start networking and building a profile, and to begin with, we are going to talk headshots.

ACT ONE

CHAPTER ONE

Headshots

During my time as a casting director, I saw a lot of amazing and terrible headshots. There were certainly a few where the person could have worn more clothing. I've seen it all, including pictures of people with a snapchat dog nose or bunny ears. Perhaps they were trying to come across as fun, but they looked ridiculous and, truly, you need to take this task seriously. Your headshot is essentially how you will make your first impression.

What is a headshot?

Typically, a headshot is a portrait photograph showing the actor's head and shoulders. The head should fill the frame and give an agent or casting director a clear view of your features, particularly your eyes, which should have within them your personality and energy. If you're getting headshots taken professionally, get a body shot done while you're at it. The whole point of a body shot is to give an agent or casting director a full picture of you. You want your body shot to capture your frame from at least above the knee. Don't stuff your hands in your pockets. You can have your hands on your hips or just hook your thumbs in your pockets with your fingers out.

Do you really need headshots?

Think of your headshot as your brand or logo. They help casting directors make quick decisions about who they might want to see more of. This is especially true when the role they're casting requires an actor with a particular look. You aren't guaranteed a role because you match the look a casting director is looking for, but you have no chance of getting it if you haven't taken headshots at all. You just won't get a look in.

Back in the day, actors walked around with printed copies of their headshots. They took them to every audition and meeting. These days, everything is digital, and people are reluctant to print things unless they have to. However, handing over a headshot with your CV and a little treat like a chocolate bar or a donut each time you see a casting director or potential agent could help you stand out in an online world. It wouldn't hurt to keep some in your car, and you can gauge whether to hand over something physical. If you're hungry for work, then you'll be looking for an edge, anything that makes you memorable in a sea of hopeful actors.

Agents and casting directors see a lot of headshots daily. They don't have time to meet with every actor trying to contact them, and taking a quick look at their headshot might be all the time they can spare. If your headshots impress, there's a chance they'll take a peek at your showreel (which we cover in chapter four).

Using a professional photographer

If you have the means to use a professional photographer, then go for it. Remember, each photographer usually has a speciality. A photographer who takes wedding photos might be very nice and artistic, but do they know that black and white photos (although stunning) do nothing to help a casting director looking for a person with red hair? Everyone had black and white headshots before digital cameras came on the market in the early 2000s. Now colour photos are what's expected.

No matter where you are in the world, a photographer who specialises in headshots for actors should know the local industry requirements, which can vary. That means they'll know the right composition, editing, lighting, colouring and sizing of the photo. Everyone likes to look their best in a photo, but resist the temptation to have your images photoshopped to remove wrinkles or moles. You don't want a photographer who creates an amazing version of you; you want a photographer who can capture the amazing you as you are.

Take the time to research photographers before you pick one. Check out their portfolios and ask actor friends for referrals. Also, look at the websites of local agents to see what's expected and to get a good idea of the look and feel you need to replicate.

Personally, I like to use photographers who shoot indoors at venues with lots of natural light; because your skin tone can appear lighter or darker than it actually is when studio lights are used. Taking your picture in a beautiful garden or on a picturesque beach will take the focus off you. If you have to be outside for the photoshoot, find a spot with a blank background, like a brick wall.

You want to find a photographer who makes you feel comfortable and also takes amazing pictures. Most charge by the hour and by the number of looks you want to capture. Others charge per session. Have a discussion upfront about the cost, and ask if they include editing and retouching as part of their price. You should end up with four to six headshots, each presenting you in a slightly different way.

Doing it yourself

I appreciate that not everyone has the budget to spend on a professional photographer. It's not essential to use one. If you decide to DIY your headshots, please do not send an agent or casting director a selfie, no matter how well you think you can take them. Invest time into learning how to take your own headshot. Find a blank wall at home (white is preferable), make yourself presentable and take the photo on your camera or phone using the timer function.

Headshot tutorial

If you plan on asking a friend to take the photo for you, find someone with a good eye. You can tell almost straightaway when a photo has been taken by someone with no idea what a headshot is supposed to look like. Sometimes, the photos are blurry, overexposed, airbrushed or harsh studio lighting is used. Other times, the photos have distracting backgrounds or even have other people in them. The point I'm making is there is some skill involved in taking a great headshot. It helps if the person taking it understands lighting, positioning and how to direct you so your facial expressions are authentic and natural. And for the love of God, do not use a filter.

Once you get an agent, it's possible they'll want you to get some professional shots done. They might even have someone they like to use for all their actors.

Components of a good headshot

There is a lot more to a headshot than a click of a camera. A bit of planning is required regarding how you'll present yourself, your mood and your environment. Here are the key aspects I suggest you think about:

Wardrobe

Changing your clothes for different shots is one way you can show a diverse range of looks. Try different necklines and find colours that suit your skin tone. For example, light colours on pale skin can make you look washed out. Solid colours are the best. I recommend getting a photo of yourself in a white top and a black top. You don't have to stick to black and white for all of your photos, but they are good base colours to start with in my opinion. You can choose clothing with subtle patterns; just don't choose anything too distracting to the eye, such as bold stripes or anything with lots of different colours. You want the most captivating thing in the picture to be your face. Never do headshots in a hat and sunglasses.

Hair and make-up

Don't wear heavy make-up and fancy hairdos. An agent or casting director wants to see YOU, and they can't see you under layers of foundation. Fix your hair and put a bit of make-up on if you want to, but keep it light. Overall, you want to make an effort to look nice without overdoing it. When your future agent sends your headshot to a casting director and they ask you to audition, they'll be expecting the person in the headshot to show up.

Timing is everything

When do you feel the most relaxed and fresh? That's when you take these photos. Is it after you've been to the gym and showered? Maybe it's after you've had a light snack and a walk?

I know life can be busy, but if you're rushing from work straight to a photoshoot, you'll turn up in a frazzled mess. I don't hold out much hope for captivating pictures in that scenario. Take the time to properly prepare for the shoot. Rearrange your schedule to remove all distractions, and book a time of day when you'll be feeling calm and focused. You want to have reserved some energy to bring to the shoot so you have life behind your eyes. If you're in a rush and thinking 'just take the damn picture', that will show up in the photo.

Versatility

There was a trend in the '80s where actors would do character shots to try to show their range. They'd dress up in costumes like a police officer or a doctor or a cowboy and sometimes do really over-the-top facial expressions. Some things deserve to stay in the '80s, and that trend is one of them. There are lots of ways to show your versatility that don't require you to go over the top. You can change your hairstyle or your clothing to show subtle distinctions. A ponytail and casual clothes in one shot, for example, and corporate clothes and straightened hair in another.

Headshot Examples

Keep it fresh

Your headshots should be updated every year or each time you change your look dramatically. So, if your headshots are of a blonde with long hair, and you are now a brunette with short hair, it's time to update the photos. There's no point in using photos from ten years ago just because you think you looked better back then than you do now. We all age and our bodies change. If you've lost a lot of weight since your last headshot was taken, it won't be a pleasant surprise for the casting team when you show up. Your body and features need to match your photo. You will only frustrate people by turning up looking completely different from your headshots. Furthermore, you actually might look perfect for a particular role right now, but you'll miss out because your headshots look like a different person. I've had to tell people at auditions "I'm sorry, you don't look like your headshot." I don't mean to be harsh, but if I don't tell them, they won't update their photo, and they'll continue to miss out on work.

Your photos need to be an authentic representation of you while also showing your versatility. Once you have them, you can use them as your profile picture on your website and social media platforms. By using different photos from the same shoot you can show some variety while simultaneously keeping a consistent look and feel. Agents or casting directors that look you up can tell easily that they're looking at the same person in each location. Haven't sorted your website and socials yet? Read on.

CHAPTER TWO

Website / Social Media

There's no getting away from it; most of the world is online, so you need to be there. Creating a website and managing social media accounts will help you promote your skills and abilities for little to no cost.

In this modern age, it's incredibly easy to set up a website and social media accounts. When I built my first website for the talent agency I started, nobody else was using them. I had to learn to write code and work out how to get everyone's images to display on this thing. I worked it out when no one else was doing it, so I have every confidence you'll be able to navigate this task with so many free online resources to guide you.

There will be a time investment required from you, not just regarding setting yourself up, but also in maintaining your online presence. So, which is more important, a website or a social media presence? The answer is both are important for different reasons, and we'll cover why next.

Your website

You might be tempted to just focus on social media and forget the website, but there are dangers in relying only on social media. These platforms are always changing in terms of the demographics that use them and their popularity. What's working well at one time might not get you anywhere in the future. Also, you can lose your social media accounts if they are hacked or someone reports you. If that happens and all your best images and videos are only on your social media, they could be lost for good. But your website belongs to you, and you have ownership of the material published on it. Social media platforms come and go, but your website will remain a steady, stable location where people can learn more about you.

There's a lot to think about when creating your website. It should be easy to find, look great and present you in the best possible way to the online world. You can build your website step by step, adding more information as you gain more experience, but the first thing to do is to choose your domain name.

Your domain name

Don't try to be cute or clever when choosing a domain name for your website. The best domain name is your name, so jump online and buy it as soon as possible, so it doesn't get purchased by someone else. You also want your social media accounts to be under your name, so don't waste time in setting those up either.

The design

Use a design that's clean and easy to navigate. If you're going to create your own website, there are plenty of free and easy to use platforms online. In the 2020s a lot of people used offerings like Wix or Weebly to build their sites; their ready-made templates have been specifically designed for easy navigation and a clean look. But technology moves fast, no doubt there will be even better 'done for you' options available in the future.

If you plan to get a bit more technical and build something custom, make sure you've taken the time to research what makes a good web layout. Remember, it's important your website looks good on a cell phone, so check that you're using a mobile-friendly design. If it all feels a bit overwhelming, you can pay someone to design it for you. The costs will vary. Make sure the person doing this for you understands your vision and the purpose of your website. Give them high quality/resolution photos and videos and the written content they'll need. Often, what holds a website up from launching is the client has not supplied these things.

Specific pages

The homepage of your website should absolutely have your most recent headshot front and centre. The second most important page for a website is your 'About' or 'Bio' page. I suggest writing this in first person to sound more personable. Ensure you have a 'Downloadables' page where you have your headshots, CV and your showreel (which we cover ahead). It's a great idea to have videos on your website of you doing some of the skills you've listed in your CV, such as playing the guitar, dancing or singing (see chapter ten – 'Develop Special Skills'). However, if you're going to showcase your talents this way, you will need to ensure you keep the videos fresh. Do not keep videos on your website of you from ten years ago. Make sure your contact details are easy to find. In the header on the home page is a good place, as well as having a 'Contact me' page.

SEO

SEO is Search Engine Optimisation. Without optimising your website for search engines, it will be virtually invisible on the Internet. Think about what words an agent or casting director might type into Google that fit your profile, e.g. 'actor', 'dancer', 'comedian' or 'Australian accent'. Ensure those keywords feature prominently and consistently throughout your website. You can also put those keywords as tags on your images. Use keywords that are unique to you and will make you stand out in a Google search, for example, 'sword fighting'. Of course, only use keywords that truly reflect your skills.

For some projects, a director will create a 'lookbook'. This is a collection of photos that communicate the look, feel and vision they have for the film and can include a particular look for specific characters. In those situations, casting directors are literally googling specific appearance characteristics to find someone with the right features to cast. That's why it's important you include keywords on your website about your appearance as well as your skills, e.g. '6 feet tall, freckles'. Make sure your name is sprinkled throughout the pages too. SEO will make it easier for people to find you, so it's worth either learning about how to do it or paying someone to do it for you. You don't want to invest a lot of time or money in creating a website that doesn't show up in search results.

Social Media Platforms

The more locations you are presented, the more accessible you are to the people searching for information about you. However, there is no point in having an account on every platform if you do not have the time or energy to keep them all fresh and updated. Choose a couple and focus on presenting yourself really well. Each platform offers something different. Let's take a closer look at some of the most commonly used platforms by actors:

Instagram

Instagram was created as a photo-sharing social media platform in 2010. As the years passed, video became king in terms of content consumption, causing platforms like Instagram to provide video sharing features such as 'reels'.

When setting up your Instagram account remember that agents and casting directors are trying to get a quick feel for who you are, so a mix of professional and personal/lifestyle posts will work well. Put your contact details in your bio. Agents and casting directors are unlikely to send you a direct message. Think carefully about what you're posting. Lots of selfies will not tell people a lot about you as a person.

In terms of what people use Instagram for, it really is where people try to present themselves in the best light possible. Posts are almost magazine in style, and the photos are strategic with filters used to give a polished look.

If you want to show a more playful side to yourself, Tiktok is probably a better location for that kind of content.

Tiktok

Tiktok is a video content platform, but it is very different from Instagram or YouTube. Videos can be uploaded or filmed on the spot and published straightaway. They are generally short, ranging from ten seconds to ten minutes. It has a unique stitch function where you can merge your video with another user's. It also has a duet option where you can put your video side by side with another user. There are lots of ways to create interesting content on Tiktok.

Here are a few suggestions:
1. Do some of your favourite scenes.
2. Do duet challenges with other actors.
3. Show off a special skill.
4. Try out some jokes.
5. Share something you learned.

Musicians are using Tiktok to get their music out to the masses. Actors can also use Tiktok to build a following and gain interest from agents and casting directors. Do something nobody else is doing, and see if you go viral. It's worth a shot. My Accent Queen Tiktok videos are quite niche and have done very well.

Accent Queen Video

Eliana Ghen has also had amazing success on Tiktok. Check out her material. If you really want to see an actor having fun on TikTok, check out Nicholas Flannery.

Actors who've gone viral on TikTok

X (formerly known as Twitter)

Sometimes called a micro-blogging social media platform, a tweet can only be a few hundred characters long. So, whatever you post, it needs to be to the point. This is a place where you can start a conversation about topics relevant to the acting profession. You don't have to be talking (or tweeting) all day; sometimes great conversation starters come from retweeting something interesting an industry leader has said. Be professional and be wary of controversy.

Threads is the competing platform for X (Twitter) and works in much the same way.

Facebook

Facebook has changed in terms of its target demographic since it was first launched in 2006. It's used less by young people than it used to be, but there are still key people in the industry using Facebook, so don't write it off.

When using Facebook, you'll need to decide if you want to create a separate 'fan page' for yourself as an actor. This will keep all your acting-specific posts separate from your personal page, where you might want to post more personal content for your friends and family. However, you don't have to create a separate public profile page. Some people just use their personal page and customise their privacy settings on each post as to whether they want it to be public and visible to anyone who might be looking them up or only visible to their friends.

If you're not going to have a separate actor's page, think about whether you want to make a post public every time you post. If you're not big on oversharing on social media, then this may not be a problem for you. Otherwise, make sure you're vigilant about it. You don't want that picture of you passed out drunk at a party accidentally being visible to everyone. However, don't get it into your head that all personal posts should be for your friends and family only. Agents and casting directors will look up your social media to get a feel for who you are as a person. So that picture of you out to lunch with your family to celebrate your mum's birthday is worth making public as long as you have the permission of the people in the photo. Also, make sure people aren't posting pictures of you without your permission. Use privacy settings that require you to approve any posts that tag you.

If it makes you nervous or you're unsure about what to make public, then you might be better off keeping your personal page personal and creating a public actor's profile page. Make sure you've put your contact information on your page and it's visible to the people looking at your profile. You will need to post regularly on it and put in the work to build a following. You might need to take a crash course in Facebook marketing to get some basic knowledge about how to help your posts reach the right people. For example, don't ask all your friends to like your page unless they will like and comment on your posts. Having a lot of people liking your page and then not engaging with it will decrease your reach.

It's your choice if you want to create a separate actor's page or use your personal profile. If you research this topic, you're likely to find articles telling you that both options are good and bad in their own ways. Whatever you decide, the most important thing is to ensure you are regularly posting pictures or videos that introduce you to the world and will give the people looking you up a good feel for who you are.

Don't forget that Facebook is also a great way to connect with fellow actors via groups or following their personal pages and/ or public profiles. Like the pages of all the agencies you're interested in connecting with. Join online communities that are sharing knowledge and opportunities.

Facebook has become a place where a lot of people share their personal views, sometimes on controversial topics. It's important you remember always that employers look up potential employees on social media, and that's true of almost all job sectors.

YouTube

YouTube is a video sharing social media platform. Videos can be long (hours if the account is verified) but when Tiktok exploded on the scene, YouTube, like Instagram, had to adapt.

They created the 'shorts' feature to allow users to quickly create bite sized videos.

There are a few reasons why actors create YouTube channels. For example, some use it as a place to keep private videos, such as footage for their showreel or audition self-tapes (I cover these in the chapters ahead). If you choose to do that, make sure your audition videos are set to private and password protected

Definitely consider using a YouTube channel as a place to promote yourself as an actor. Do the basics, such as uploading a profile pic and choosing a banner image, then choose a featured video. This will be the first video that displays on your channel homepage. Think about what you want a potential agent or casting director to see first. If you haven't got a great video to put there, create one. Your YouTube channel could be a great place to showcase your talents. Upload examples of your work and videos of your skills, such as dancing, singing, or playing musical instruments. Just make sure they're recent videos and you're actually showing off a talent, and you're not just uploading videos of you trying something.

Even if you're not planning on using a YouTube channel as a place to promote yourself, agents or casting directors may still look you up on the platform, so it's important you have a basic profile in place. Fill out the description section to introduce yourself and link it to your other social media pages and website.

YouTube is also a great place for you to learn from people within the industry. There are tons of free videos from experts giving you all sorts of tips and advice. Do double check who you're watching, though. Anyone can upload a video spouting advice, so it's worth checking their credentials.

Be strategic

Actors put a lot of work into trying to get noticed. It can be exhausting but it's been worth it for a number of well-known actors such as Andy Sandberg and Donald Glover.[1]

Actors that started on YouTube

Make sure that your social media platforms point to each other as well as your website. That way an agent or casting director who comes across you online can learn more about you quickly. There are several 'link in bio' options that send people to a page with all your socials and websites listed, such as 'linktree' or 'beacons'.

My Links Page

---

1 MsMojo (2018, November 27). *Top 10 Actors You Didn't Know Got Their Start on YouTube* [Video]. YouTube.

Once you've made it easy for them to find you, go and find them. Follow all the accounts of key contacts in the industry to keep up to date on what projects they're working on. The comments you make on their posts are more likely to be seen by them than your attempt to slide into their DMs (direct messages). Be authentic with your comments and make them about the content they've posted (instead of using it as a way to ask them to follow you or meet up). If you're sincere, they might get curious about you and look up your profile. You never know.

By the time you've read this book, another social media platform may have sprung up, more features may have been added to existing platforms, and advice about how to approach building a website may have changed. The online world is a realm that's constantly growing and changing. Essentially, my advice is applicable across all platforms, including your website. Keep it consistent, keep it fresh and keep it professional. You might really want to put someone in their place online, but it's in your best interest not to. Instead, put your effort into creating a website and social media accounts that will house examples of all the great work you've done and all the work you're going to do.

It's true that it can be difficult to land roles without an agent, but a strong social media presence can help. Heading along to open castings can also assist you as you build up a profile. Let's explore that next.

CHAPTER THREE

Open Castings

Y ou might think your next step at this point is to find an agent. Of course, getting an agent is an important milestone in an actor's career, but to be signed up to an agency, you need a solid showreel that showcases your acting ability. If you have not yet been cast in a single production or project, you will need to build up your experience to catch the eye of an agent.

Depending on the production, open castings can give actors the opportunity to get some work under their belt. When I was fifteen, I went to an open casting for an opera. It was a Benjamin Britten play called *Noye's Fludde*, and I got a part! I never thought I would get it, and I wouldn't have if I hadn't given an open casting a shot.

What is an open casting?

An open casting (or open call) is an audition that allows anyone to try out for the role regardless of experience or training. They can attract a lot of people, so expect a long queue and a long day if you decide to brave it at all.

What kind of work can you get?

All sorts! Open castings are used in theatre, film and television for many reasons. Sometimes the production team are looking for talent they haven't seen before.

The role is unlikely to be the lead, but there are some big-name projects that have used open castings for supporting roles, such as the Harry Potter and Star Wars franchises. But do unknowns really get cast? Yes, they do. James and Oliver Phelps are the twin brothers who were cast as George and Fred Weasley in the Harry Potter films. They were fourteen years old, had no acting experience and skipped school to attend an open audition for the first film, *Harry Potter and the Philosopher's Stone.[2]*

Interview with James and Oliver Phelps

In 2014, the Star Wars franchise cast two unknown actors, Pip Andersen and Crystal Clarke, in *Star Wars: Episode VII The Force Awakens*. Pip and Crystal were among the thirty-seven thousand hopeful actors who attended the open auditions for those roles.[3]

---

2 OxfordUnion. (2016, October 26). *Oliver and James Phelps | Full Q&A | Oxford Union* [Video]. YouTube.
3 Child, B. (2014, July 7). *Star Wars Episode 7 adds two more cast from open auditions.* The Guardian.

Open auditions should be approached as seriously as any other audition. You will need to have a good handle on the character you are portraying. If you are going to a theatre open casting, be prepared to do a monologue (which we cover in chapter twelve) and have a song ready if required. There are lots of online casting websites you can sign up to, like Star Now and Backstage, that list open auditions for all levels of experience.

The benefits of open castings

An open audition that has been widely advertised is likely to draw a big crowd and is sometimes referred to as a 'cattle call'. Hundreds, and sometimes thousands, of actors can line up for hours only to read one line and be sent on their way. Attending these kinds of auditions can take up a lot of time and money, especially if you have to travel a fair distance to get there. However, there are ways to make the most of these auditions, so if you're going to shoot your shot, ensure you make it count.

Meet people

Every second you spend in an 'acting situation' is another chance to network with fellow actors. You will be stuck waiting in line for a while, so strike up a conversation. What work have your line buddies done? Maybe they know about some upcoming projects or have some contacts?

Practice auditioning

Every audition is another chance to practise dealing with nerves, memorising lines and standing in front of casting directors. An open audition is a chance to throw your hat in the ring and improve your audition techniques. Remember to ensure you meet the criteria of the casting call; it is open, but only to people who meet requirements. If they are asking for people over fifty, do not go if you are thirty, thinking they can use make-up to make you look older. They expect people to read and follow the instructions of the audition call, not waste their time.

Observe

How is everyone preparing themselves? Do they know some good techniques for getting into character? If you are going to an open theatre audition, sometimes you are allowed to watch the other auditions, so that's a great opportunity to take in other performances and hear feedback.

Stay positive

When the line stretches around the corner, it might feel like a waste of time to be there, but remember, an open casting can draw a lot of people who have absolutely no acting ability at all. They saw the advertisement and thought 'I could do that'. So, although the numbers are high, the calibre could be low, so keep your head up and give it your best shot.

You might have the perfect look

If you're going to an open audition for a commercial, they sometimes have a specific brief. Some might be looking for models, but many are simply looking for everyday people. This is especially true for commercials that use storytelling as their selling mechanism. They want the people watching their commercial to see themselves in it. That means they will be looking for people from all walks of life and with all body shapes and ages. So, if you fit the brief (and the brief could be anything from tall, short, young or old), then you've got a good chance of being cast. If you have the right look and can follow directions, they will make it work.

If you don't have the look the casting director is looking for, you are probably NOT going to get the role. You might meet the casting specifications by changing your hair or wardrobe, but sometimes you're not going to meet the criteria no matter what you do.

This is especially true if they're looking for specific features, e.g. small nose or round face. In those cases, it won't matter if you do an Oscar-worthy audition, as the right look will take precedence over everything else (on most occasions).

What to watch out for

There are some less-than-reputable people out there who know all too well how eager some actors are to land roles and realise their dreams. Since you are navigating auditions without an agent, you will need to use your street smarts to work out who is offering a bona fide opportunity and who is just looking for suckers. There are plenty of open castings that are authentic, so don't write them all off as dodgy, just take the time to look into:

Who are these people?

Jump on the net and sleuth. Check out the production company's website. What other work have they done? What is the name of the contact person associated with the casting and the people behind the production company itself? What's their work history? Are they associated with people recognised within the industry? If your research hasn't given you much, ask around on local actor Facebook groups or within your circle of connections to see if anyone has heard of the people involved.

Are they going to pay you?

Low-budget productions are more likely to do open castings. They may be on the lookout for newbie actors who will work for experience. You must decide for yourself if you will do that. Some scammers have even tried to convince actors to pay to be cast in their project; if that happens to you…run.

Be safe

If you're still not one hundred percent on whether the audition is legit, take a friend with you to your audition, or at the very least, tell a friend or family member where and when your audition is. You could make plans to meet up with someone after your audition as an added security measure.

Check your contract

When I was running my talent agency, one actor on my books saw an open casting for a commercial and auditioned and got the part. I required my clients to let me know if they got work elsewhere, so he brought me the contract, and it wasn't good. Thankfully, I could negotiate him a better deal, but he was lucky. Many actors starting out will go into open castings completely unaware of clauses that cut them out of big money and allow their image to be used over and over for nothing. If you don't protect your physical image, your face could end up being sold to one of the big stock-image libraries and used in advertising by big-name companies without you seeing a cent. Definitely look out for perpetuity clauses, which will give advertisers the right to use your image forever, and worldwide usage clauses, which will let them use your advertisement worldwide for no additional compensation. I cover contracts more deeply in chapter twenty-one.

More on commercials

As I said before, open castings are used for theatre, films and television shows, but if you are starting out as an actor, you may find commercials are one of the more common open castings you'll come across.

Many well-known actors started off doing commercials. It is heartening to know they were once very much like the rest of us, taking whatever opportunities came their way. Here is a list of some you can find on YouTube:

Paul Rudd - Nintendo
Keanu Reeves - Kellogg's cornflakes
Steve Carell - Brown's chicken
Brad Pitt – Pringles[4]

---

4 WatchMojo. (2014, February14). *Top 10 Celebrity Commercials from Before They Were Stars* [Video]. YouTube.

Famous Actors in Commercials

However, it's important to remember that those commercials were unlikely to have been their big break, and your commercial roles are unlikely to be yours. They served as a stepping stone on a learning journey, which is how commercial work should be viewed (in my opinion), as a chance to grow and learn.

You may hear from some people that doing commercial work can hurt your chances of landing more serious acting roles. Some actors do a few commercials, quite enjoy the work and choose to stay in that world (which can pay quite well for large-name advertisers). Some become a household figure for a brand and only do commercials for them. When you get to that status, it's unlikely you will get any other kind of work. You won't be cast in a movie if the director is concerned you'll be recognised as the 'cold and cough drops' guy. That's not to say you shouldn't do commercials at all, but be aware that you could start being recognised as a commercial actor after you've done a few.

Whether you will land roles via open castings is not something you can predict, but one thing you can be sure of is that each open casting will be an opportunity for you to listen, learn and grow. The professionals running an open casting are looking for talent, but they're also observing who is on time, takes direction and shows promise. If you're not a fit for the audition, but you did a good job, a casting director might file you in the back of their mind for a future role. It doesn't matter if the role you land was an open casting; a role is a role, and if you're saying lines (even if it's only one), you'll have something to put on your showreel. If open castings are not working out for you, you can still work on putting a showreel together. Let's look at how next.

CHAPTER FOUR

Your Showreel

You might think it's best to wait a bit longer before you make your showreel. Maybe you want better footage, to have completed more training or lost some weight? I assure you, the best time to do your showreel is now. The chance to grab the attention of a casting director or agent could happen at any time. It's important you have something to show them.

If you are still collecting footage for your showreel, just use what you have, intending to swap it out later. Originally, I had clips from a commercial I did with the New Zealand netball team on my showreel because it was fun and entertaining. As I completed more projects, my commercial work fell off my reel in place of better acting examples. Consider how much depth you presented in the work you've done and decide for yourself if it's the best you can offer for your showreel right now. It might be, and that's okay.

What is a showreel?

A showreel is a short collection of footage that takes the viewer on a journey through an actor's career and experience. It plays a vital role in helping you get an agent and in securing auditions after that.

Components of a good showreel

Ahead, we'll dive into the different acting examples you could include on your showreel, but first, let's look at some crucial elements that will help your showreel shine.

A beginning, middle and end

Insert a title card at the beginning with your name and your agent's name if you have one. You could also put your headshot. Then go straight into the best footage you have of your acting. You have thirty seconds at the most to make a good impression, so forget the idea of having a stunning finale; put all your best stuff upfront. At the end of the reel, put your contact details.

Less is more

Three minutes is the absolute maximum length of a showreel. If you don't have a lot of quality clips, don't try and stretch them out by using filler shots. You want it short, sweet and fantastic! A shorter reel with good footage is much better than something long and underwhelming. They want to see what you're capable of as quickly as possible.

It's up to date

Your showreel needs to be as fresh in terms of content as it can be. If you haven't done any work recently, then just use whatever your last work was. I'm talking about work you've done as an adult. There's no point using any work you did as a child unless, of course, you are still a child. Put footage on your showreel that shows YOU as you are NOW. What you've done recently is more relevant than what you did ten years ago.

Show some variety

If all of your clips have the same look, feel, storyline and emotion, your showreel may come across as a little monotonous. Hopefully, you have different clips of you showing a range of characteristics and emotions. Mix them up so the viewer can see different sides of you and isn't seeing more of the same.

Forget doing a montage of quick shots

Like character headshots, montages of a tiny clips were big in the '80s, and that's the only time they were acceptable on a showreel. Distracting music with footage of you making dramatic entrances and exits from scenes will get your showreel switched off before it even gets going. It might look cool, but quick tiny clips of your close ups tell an agent or casting director very little about your acting ability.

Edit it well

If you've gone to the effort of collating amazing footage of your acting abilities, don't let yourself down with poor editing. An agent or casting director has seen countless showreels. They have seen the good, the bad and the ugly. If you think there's a corner you can cut that they won't notice, you're kidding yourself.

There are a lot of factors to consider when editing clips together, from smooth transitioning to picture quality and effective pace. Your showreel should move through different scenes without distracting or confusing the viewer. If you have any budget at all for your showreel, paying someone to edit the clips together might be a good idea. If you have no choice but to do this part yourself, then at the very least, take the time to do some research and effectively take a crash course in editing. Ensure you put some text at the bottom of each scene to credit where it has come from or put a title card before each clip.

My Showreel

What to include on your showreel

Do a stocktake of what footage you have. Is it enough to make a compelling showreel? If you haven't got much to work with, start with what you've got and build on it.

Featured extra work

If you have lines or even only one line in a television show or film, use a screen recorder, such as Loom or Quicktime, and pop it on your showreel. This is something worth including.

However, if your only task as an extra was to walk from one side of the room to the other, I'm sorry; that footage will not convince anyone of your acting abilities. You might have been walking with great determination and gusto, but truthfully, if you were noticeable as a background extra, you weren't doing your job very well.

Generally, background talent / extra footage is not appropriate for your showreel. During my time as an agent and also when I was a casting director, I received showreels where people had added in red arrows or circles to help the viewer locate them in the scene. I'm trying to gauge your acting ability, not play 'Where's Waldo?'

Don't get me wrong, background extras are an important part of the acting world. They help create a believable environment for actors to work within. Doing background talent work can be a helpful part of your acting journey, and I discuss this more in chapter six 'Working as an Extra'.

Music Videos

Some actors include work they've done on music videos if it tells a story. It will be up to you to decide whether you showcased acting skills in the music video. If you were just dancing around in the background, maybe leave it out.

Commercials

Like with music videos, consider whether the commercial you were in showcases your acting abilities. There are some fantastic commercials out there, and they have their own awards at the Emmys, so there's every chance your commercial work is brilliant. But if your commercial work required little depth in your expression, consider what you could add to your showreel to show more range.

A monologue

Preferably, an agent or casting director would like to see how you react to other actors and how you present yourself in a scene. But if you are starting from scratch and have limited footage, self-taping a monologue may be a good option to give them something rather than nothing. Check out chapter eighteen to learn more about self-taping.

I cover monologues in more detail in chapter twelve, but in short, it is important to choose a scene and character you can relate to and is similar to you in age and identity. You don't have to limit yourself in terms of skill, definitely choose a scene that shows you can act your way out of a paper bag.

I recommend you stay away from famous scenes likely to result in you being compared to an Oscar-winning actor. Choose a scene that is more obscure and less likely to result in the viewer comparing your performance to the one they have in their memory banks. A scene like that is also less likely to be something they're sick to death of seeing. However, if you are set on doing a famous scene, bring all your skills to it and find a way to make the scene your own instead of an impersonation

Join an existing project

On any given day, there's a student film or low budget short film looking for actors willing to work for experience. Ask your local acting community to see what projects are out there. It needs to have a great script and provide you with a chance to showcase your acting skills.

Creating footage for your showreel

If you can't find a project to join and all you have to put on your showreel is a monologue, you need to get to work creating your own acting footage. An actor is an artist; you're imaginative and creative. It's time to give script writing a go and direct your own scenes. You don't have to do a whole film for a showreel, just do a couple of scenes and do them well.

Think about the different roles you'd be perfect for. Do you want to do a girlfriend/boyfriend scene, a mum/dad scene, a psycho killer scene? Many would caution actors to stick to believable roles when shooting your showreel. But what is believable in a world of make believe? The actors in *Avatar* didn't know they'd be perfect as blue people with tails, and I'm sure the actors in *The Hobbit* didn't know they'd be amazing as short hairy people.

It's your showreel. You can choose to take risks with it or not. My dream role would be a gun-toting, badass b#tch. I would love to be that character, but unless Simon Pegg does a sequel to *Hot Fuzz*, I wouldn't put that sort of footage on my showreel. That's just me, though, and as I said before, each actor will need to decide for themselves what scenes they'd like to shoot for their showreel. If you're dead set on getting a particular outside-the-box role, then film it for your showreel and make it believable. You don't want the casting director to experience second-hand embarrassment from watching your work.

Finding equipment

If renting a camera and sound gear is outside your budget, you might be able to find some people who own the equipment and are looking for ways to build up their experience. If you find such generous souls, think about ways you can show your appreciation, from giving a little money or even just buying everyone lunch.

If you can't access the required gear, you'll have to work with what you've got. Most smartphones have a good-enough camera to capture what you need. Look online, where no doubt you'll find some good tips about how to film scenes on a shoestring budget.

Your scene partner(s)

If you're filming your own scenes, then you get to be the casting director. If you have some actor contacts, choose someone you work well with and can enjoy shooting with. If you have to choose between shooting a scene with an experienced actor or someone who has trouble remembering their lines, I strongly suggest you choose someone who is going to make the scene look good. It will not be convincing at all if you've asked your mate to say the lines, and they just stand there, reading from a page. For it to look professional, you'll need to work with someone with acting skills. If you're worried they might be better than you, then you'll just have to work extra hard to present at their level. The last thing you want an agent or casting director to remember about your showreel is how bad the person across from you was. Outshine your fellow actor, but you definitely don't want them to steal the show for all the wrong reasons.

Using a showreel production company

In some parts of the world you can approach a showreel production company to assist you in creating your showreel. Some will help you shoot footage if you don't have much, but this will not be cheap. They arrange the scripts and actors for you to shoot with and can help put it all together. If you have the means, then there's no reason why you couldn't take this route.

Showreel Companies

Here are a couple of things to check when looking for a showreel production company:

Mind the bells and whistles

Look at what they've created for other people and get some reviews and feedback from other actors. Some companies use expensive equipment and software to create something that has so many bells and whistles that it's all you can see and hear. You want an agent or casting director to be captivated by your acting and not be highly aware of any visual or sound effects.

Do their showreels all look the same?

They might have a list of core scenes/scripts they use for all of their clients, causing their showreels to look similar. This is something casting directors will notice.

Do they offer an in-between option?

For example, you might have some actor friends who will shoot scenes with you for free, but you might pay the showreel company to capture the footage for you to ensure you get a professional look. Or you might do everything yourself and then pay them to tidy it up at the end. As long as the final product looks professional and showcases you to the best of your ability, then it doesn't matter how you got it to that point.

Remember, your showreel is an ever-changing showcase. It's not something you're stuck with, so don't hesitate. Make a start; it will only improve as you gain more experience. Filming your own footage for your showreel shows you are driven and have determination; and maybe, just maybe, you've stumbled upon a new passion.

CHAPTER FIVE

Making Your Own Movies

I f filming your own scenes for your showreel didn't drive you to tears, then you may have discovered a hidden talent. I personally enjoyed the screenwriting process and learned a lot from giving it a go. I wrote a screenplay called *Hobnail Boots*, which was about a group of wacky characters who went on all sorts of adventures across New Zealand. I wrote it with Tom Sainsbury, who is an amazing actor, writer and director. We got close to having it made and even had Antony Starr (now known from *The Boys* TV series) come and read for us, but, alas, we never got the greenlight.

How can making your own movies help you as an actor?

One of the great things about making your own short film is that it's something you can do right now. Your first attempts might not be your greatest work, but you'll soon pick up techniques to improve your filmmaking. You'll also gain an appreciation for the work that goes into writing a great script and learn how to best capture acting on film. Here are some more great reasons why making your own movies can help you in your acting journey.

You can take your career into your own hands

A triple threat in the industry used to be known as a singer, dancer, actor. In modern times, actors who write their own scripts, create their own films and star in them are considered by some to be the new triple threat (writer, director, actor).[5]

There have been many actors who, when they became frustrated with waiting for someone to pick them, decided to pick themselves. They took pen to paper, wrote a script, grabbed a camera and got on with starring in their own films.

This isn't to say that you wouldn't continue to audition or look for an agent. Working on a passion project while continuing to search for roles can help actors feel empowered. This can be important at a time when the decisions affecting your career are, for the most part, out of your hands.

Matt Damon and Ben Affleck often share in interviews that their Academy Award-winning script Good Will Hunting was an attempt to gain some career control. They had been landing small parts but hadn't been able to break through into the lead roles they wanted. Matt spoke about this on the Rosie O'Donnell Show in 1997 when he was interviewed about the project: 'We were unemployed and we were broke. We were just looking for jobs so we kind of created this thing to give ourselves jobs.'[6]

5 Gilliss, G. (2021, May 13). Be the New Triple Threat: Actor-Writer-Producer. Backstage.
6 Rosie O'Donnell. (2022, September 8). Matt Damon Interview – ROD Show, Season 2 Episode 63, 1997 [Video]. YouTube.

Matt Damon Interview

You can create your dream role

Most people know of Taika Waititi as the director of famous films including *Thor Ragnarok* and *Jojo Rabbit*, and he is, indeed, a highly regarded director. He is also an actor. He started his filmmaking career by shooting short films for a 48-hour film contest in New Zealand, which he also starred in.[7] Since 2004, Taika has produced nineteen films and cast himself as an actor in many of them (not always as the lead, but sometimes).[8] We can't all be Taika Waititi; he is one in a million, that's for sure; but there's a lot to be learned from his journey. He wanted to act, and he wanted to make films, so he did both, and he does both brilliantly.

It's your script and your movie. You can write a fantastic character for yourself, someone you've always wanted to play. You have poetic licence to tell a story you've always wanted to tell. So, take the chance to let your creativity run wild and write a script that lets your acting strengths shine through.

---

7 NZ On Screen. (2023, April 3). *Taika Waititi*.
8 Taika Waititi. Credits. IMDb.

You could be a great director and not know it

Being an actor can strengthen your abilities as a director because you can relate directly to your actor's experience. You will hopefully have a good understanding of what they need from you to deliver the scene. You know what it's like to be vulnerable as an actor, and so you'll have a greater level of empathy for your actors when they need to access deep emotions. Of course, you'll also be aware of camera angles, entry points and exit points, etc., but a director who understands the needs of an actor will ensure they haven't overlooked the crucial part they play in the production.

Starting a movie project

If you're feeling inspired, that's great! But before you dive in, remember it's important you take your film project seriously. Here are a few important points to remember when making your own movies:

Getting the script right

If you're going to put the time and effort into creating your own movie, you at least want to ensure you have considered all the necessary components. This might mean taking your script to different people for feedback. Look into what makes a great script. Does your dialogue need work? Are your characters well rounded? Once you've written your movie, sit down with a group of people/actors and read through the whole movie to hear what it sounds like, because inevitably you will want to make changes. Work out your storyboard and have a play with filming different scenes. Make sure your actors are rehearsing (you included), so when the camera is rolling, you're getting the goods. Filming sessions are not the time to rehearse. Everyone is volunteering their time to do this thing, and their time is valuable.

Get the right equipment

Whether you rent it, buy it or borrow it, make sure you've got the right equipment, especially for lighting and sound. The amazing acting you capture will be all for nothing if no one can see or hear the actors. To source this equipment, start with your own network of actor friends. You could put a flyer up at your local film school to see if there is anyone who wants to join the project and gain some experience. Hopefully, you'll connect with people who have skills and equipment or know how to find it.

Consider learning from professionals

Experimenting with filmmaking will help you learn about the behind-the-camera skills required, but to speed things up, you might like to learn from the professionals. There are lots of options, from in-person filmmaking courses to online tutorials and books. The things you'll learn about lighting, sound and camera technique may save you having to reshoot material in the future and will give you the confidence to start.

Think about your budget

Low-budget films do not necessarily mean low quality. Lots of filmmakers have found innovative ways to keep costs low while also creating a high-quality film. For example, there have been some incredible films shot entirely on an iPhone, such as *High Flying Bird* directed by Steven Soderbergh.[9]

It could be that the story is told almost entirely in one location or even in only a few rooms. A great script and amazing acting will keep the audience engaged. You only need to watch a movie like *Reservoir Dogs* to see how it's done. Sometimes actors play multiple roles as another cost-saving option. You might have to put your thinking cap on and be creative. If there's any budget at all, ensuring you have good sound and post production editing can be a real lifesaver.

Find the right people

Most of us know how important a team dynamic is when working on a project. It's as true on a film set as it is in an office. Choosing the right team could make or break your project. You want people who are as motivated as you to complete the film. If all of you are hoping for a career in the film and television industry, then doing a really good job on this project will serve everyone well. Choose people who you get along with and who you know to be committed and hard working. If your script writing isn't strong, find a writing partner to take the pressure off and to help you work in a more collaborative way.

With the right team, you could end up working on multiple projects together and find success as a team. Kevin Smith started his filmmaking career making *Clerks* for $27,575 USD. He brought in people he connected with on a short filmmaking course to do the technical work and cast friends such as Jason

---

9 Lindbergh, B. (2019, Feb 7). *The Rise of the iPhone* Auteur. The Ringer.

Mewes to act. Kevin went on to direct several films with the same people. If you find a good thing, why change it?[10]

Film festivals

Should you submit your project to film festivals or online competitions? Yes, do it! What have you got to lose? There are thousands of film festivals worldwide, but you won't be eligible for all of them. Take the time to check submission requirements. There is often a fee and other costs involved. If you have big dreams of premiering via the Sundance or the Cannes Film Festival, make sure you've checked that your film meets all their specifications and you have the budget to meet the associated costs. For example, if your film is selected to premiere, you'll need to meet the travel cost of going to the festival. Don't give up if you're not accepted. According to www.sundance.org, there were 14,849 films submitted from around the world for the Sundance Festival in 2022, of which 84 feature-length and 59 short films were accepted.[11] It's a tall order to make it, but if you're dead set on trying, then back yourself; you've got zero chance if you don't submit. There are plenty of smaller, less well-known film festivals that you can submit to also if you want to start smaller and build your way up to bigger possibilities.

Premiere

You can also choose to upload it to your website and launch the film yourself online. Make the Internet your premiere platform if you want to and market yourself to a global audience. Just remember, the Internet

---

10 Kevin Smith. (2015, December 28). *22 years ago, I sent this incomplete budget along with a copy of #Clerks to @miramax in hopes they'd buy my flick.* [Image attached] [Status update]. Facebook.
11 Sundance Film Festival 2022 At-A-Glance. Film submissions. Sundance.

is a big place. A lot of filmmakers are trying to grab the attention of the world online, so it's not a platform without competition.

Don't forget, you also have your local community to promote your film to. You could hold an in-person premiere at your local theatre and invite the media, casting directors and agents to attend along with all the friends and family of your crew. If that's too costly, you could see if there are any arts grants available to cover the cost or fundraise to make it happen.

Making films has all kinds of benefits in terms of what you could learn, who you could meet and how you might gain a profile. But it's no small task. It should definitely be something you feel excited and passionate about doing. If you're interested, but feel like it's something you couldn't take on yourself, you can always look for someone doing an interesting project and ask to join. That way you could still learn from the filmmaking process but not have the pressure sitting entirely on your shoulders. Or you can learn about film sets and how they work simply by doing some extra work.

CHAPTER SIX

Working as an Extra

Extra work, like movie making, is something you can do right now; you do not need to have an agent to do it. You might consider joining an agency specifically for background talent (which I'll cover ahead), but you don't have to.

My first paid acting work was as a background extra on a British police TV series called *The Bill*. I was cast as 'girl on bus', and I was super excited and star struck to be working on a real television set. I worked hard all day acting my heart out as 'girl on bus', but when I sat down to watch the episode, it turned out that I was in fact 'foot on bus'. That was what my effort had amounted to: a foot. They say you have to start somewhere, and well, for me, I started as a foot. Despite the disappointment, I still had a great day working with other extras and enjoying the buzz and hum of a working television set.

What is a background extra?

Let's say you're watching a movie, and the lead actors are talking to each other while walking down a city street. Would you believe this conversation was taking place in a busy city if there weren't people walking along the footpath in the background? Or what if you were watching a scene where the lead actors are having dinner in a completely empty restaurant? That would look very strange indeed. The empty environment would probably distract you from the story they're trying to tell. The people sitting at the tables around the lead actors are extras, and their performance in the background creates an authentic environment so you, as the viewer, can concentrate on the story being told.

Background extra roles are non-speaking and generally attract little to no attention. They create a believable environment for lead actors to work within.

An extra is sometimes referred to as:
'Background talent'
'Background actor'
'Supporting artist'
'Non-speaking performer'

In this chapter, I am not talking about 'featured extras', who may say a few words or perform a task in front of the camera. I am specifically referring to the people who fill the background of a scene to give it depth and realism.

The benefits of background extra work

There are definitely a lot of benefits in doing background extra work when you're starting out as an actor, but let me be clear, it is highly unlikely that you will get an agent or the attention of a casting director this way. So why would you do it? Well, let's take a look at some reasons:

It's a learning experience

Stepping on set for the first time can be daunting. Doing background extra work is a way to ease yourself into the environment like a fly on the wall. It gives you a chance to watch closely how a scene is filmed. What directions are being given to the lead actors? How are things run? Not only can you learn a lot from watching amazing actors at work, you can also learn about the inner workings of a shoot and on-set etiquette. You'll see how people from different professions relate and communicate with each other. Who reports to who? How are challenges resolved? Observe the use of cameras and lighting. Take it all in.

Earn while you learn

There aren't many learning environments out there where you are paid while you learn. It is considered entry-level work, however, and the pay level generally reflects that. Background extras are sometimes undervalued in my opinion, especially when you consider they are essential for most scenes to work in movies and television.

In countries with actor unions, there are minimum standards of payment and conditions for background extras, which is a relief. There is some danger of mistreatment of background extras in countries where such protections do not exist. It can be long days and hard work for minimal pay, so consider it like an apprenticeship and take advantage of the chance to learn.

Meet people

It doesn't matter if you're only on set as a background extra, if you're there, you're there, and you will be surrounded by other actors and professionals in the business. This is not your big chance to get in the ear of the director, but it is a chance for you to meet and connect with other potential contacts. From the costume team to the make-up artist or the runner, whoever you might come into contact with as part of your work is someone you should genuinely get to know. You never know who has information about an upcoming project or knows a great tip about the industry.

Joining a background talent agency

To ensure you get paid fairly, sign up with a background talent agency that specialises in sourcing background extras. Not only will working with a background extras agency ensure you get paid adequately, they will also ensure other aspects are agreed, such as overtime, breaks and meals. If you are asked to say lines on set, you can contact your agency, and they will upgrade your contract to reflect the change in terms of payment.

A background talent agency will ask what kind of physical activity you'll be required to do and ensure you get paid accordingly. For example, if a nightclub scene takes all day to shoot, you could spend the whole day dancing in the background. For that kind of work, you need to be paid more than an extra who had to sit in a cafe in the background all day.

Can extra work hurt your career?

Some people may warn you against signing with a background talent agency because an acting agent could be less likely to sign you on to their books if you are not a completely 'fresh face'. I still think doing extra work is beneficial, especially for new actors learning about the biz. Here are some suggestions and points to consider regarding extra work:

Keep your head down and your back to the camera

As an actor, it may feel counterintuitive to shrink away from the spotlight, but I advise trying to stay in the wings when it comes to background extra work. This is not the time to try to 'be discovered', it's an opportunity to learn. In small countries, the movie/television industry is more likely to be a close-knit community, so you may find it harder to hide your extra work history. But in larger countries, where the industry is more widespread, an agent is unlikely to know that you have worked with a background extra agency unless you tell them.

If you're concerned that an agent will find out you're on the books for a background talent agency, you could go for background extra work only offered via open castings (which we covered in chapter three). But keep in mind, if you're a part of a small community, you may still be recognised at an open casting.

You are at risk of being featured

Being a background extra will teach you a lot fast. But if you are hopeful of auditioning for a role on a series you are currently an extra on, being plucked from the background to be a featured extra could ruin your chances.

This can happen on any set where you are working as a background extra. At any point, the director may pluck you from the crowd and ask you to say a line. If that happens, you have no choice in the matter. Saying 'no thanks' is a one-way ticket to the exit. A featured extra will say up to five words; beyond that, you will be upgraded to a small-part performer contract. This will mean an increase in pay, which is great, but now that you have been featured, you may not be brought back as an extra again.

If you end up being upgraded to a featured extra or a small-part performer, you'll need to find a way to make it work to your advantage. If you have an agent, contact them as soon as you can to talk about getting a screen credit. At the very least, you'll have something to add to your CV and showreel.

Be honest

You do not have to put your background extra work on your resume, and actually, it's recommended that you don't, as it tells agents and casting directors little about your abilities as an actor. If you were a featured extra, you might pop that on your CV as 'lady behind counter', etc., but if you were just 'man crossing road in the background', definitely leave it out.

Don't try to pass your background extra work off as principal acting roles. Name dropping that you were in a movie walking behind Jennifer Aniston will not impress. Reputation is everything in this business, and one small lie in one area can put the rest of your legitimate hard work into disrepute.

Do you want to stay in the background?

Doing a lot of background extra work will, in time, earn you a reputation as a professional background extra actor. There's nothing wrong with that, and many people make a living this way. Jesse Heiman is a well-known background extra who became an Internet sensation when a montage of all the films and television shows he could be seen in did the rounds on the Internet[12] He went on to star in a Super Bowl commercial, so being a background extra worked out well for him.

---

12 ABC News. (2013, February 2). *Hollywood's Favorite Extra in GoDaddy Super Bowl Ad* [Video]. YouTube.

Jesse Heiman Background Extra

When I was an agent for background extras, productions would call me up and ask for particular extras by name. That's because these people had earned a reputation as dependable extras who followed directions well.

If it's not your intention to only do background extra acting, then it's best to limit this kind of work as a learning experience you do a handful of times at the beginning of your career while continuing to put effort into getting an agent and principal roles.

On-set etiquette

You might feel a little star struck on set. It's pretty amazing to be so close to the people who make or break careers. But remember, this is a time to observe and learn, not schmooze and self-promote.

Don't pester people

Of course, you'll have instructions to follow and work to do on the day, but depending on the project, you might find yourself with a bit of downtime. This is not your chance to introduce yourself to the assistant director or ask the lead actor for a selfie.

Extras can sometimes be put out when the lead actor won't talk to them or they seem to hide in their trailer. Remember, a lead actor has a lot on their plate and needs space to remain in character or go over lines.

Keep things confidential

Whether you're on a movie set or a television series, do not be tempted to post anything online about what you saw or heard on set. You won't do yourself any favours if you get a reputation as the extra who gave away a plot twist or casting secret. You could also find yourself in serious legal trouble, especially if you signed a confidentiality agreement.

Have a search on YouTube and you'll find plenty of videos of well-known actors doing background extra work, from Bruce Willis and Renee Zellweger to Jackie Chan and Ben Affleck.[13] It's true that many famous actors started out doing extra work, but it's important to note that these actors did not become famous because of their extra work. They were learning on set, just like you're going to.

Famous Actors as Extras

---

13 WhatCulture. (2021, September 26). *10 Huge Actors You Didn't Notice As Extras in Movies* [Video]. YouTube.

Extra work can be a great way to check out how film and television sets work, but don't mistakenly think that background extra work is your ticket to fame. It's your ticket to learning and joining in the industry. If you don't like the idea of staying in the shadows and think you might be ready for the spotlight, you won't find a brighter spotlight than the one pointed at stand-up comedians. Think you might be game? Read ahead.

CHAPTER SEVEN

Stand-Up Comedy

I love to make people laugh. It's like creating fire. When you get that first chuckle, that's the spark, and you have to be quick-witted to stay on a roll and keep it burning. Many times, I'd go to parties and have the whole room in stitches, so I decided to give stand-up comedy a go. I went along to an open mic night, but when I got there, I froze in terror. I just couldn't make myself do it. It's not until you're there that you realise how truly vulnerable comedians are when they deliver their material. They may look like they've just walked on stage and are having a chat with the audience, but really, they've taken months and months to perfect their set. They've considered every line, every word and every pause. It's constructed but also leaves room for improvisation.

What is stand-up comedy?

Stand-up comedy is a live comedic performance performed in front of an audience. It requires actors to draw on a set of skills, such as timing, improvisation and observation. If you're doing a set as part of a line-up, most comedians need to have enough material to cover about fifteen minutes.

How can stand-up comedy help you as an actor?

There's no question that stand-up comedy requires a certain level of bravery, but if you can summon that courage, there's a lot to gain from giving stand-up comedy a proper chance.

Before you decide that you couldn't possibly be bold enough to do stand-up comedy, have a think about the acting work you've done already. Have you acted in some roles that required you to access deep emotions? I'm sure you have. You probably had to act in front of people while sitting in those deep emotions too. So, you already know how to allow yourself to experience vulnerability.

Perhaps you felt safer in those situations because it was a closed set or you were with a group on stage? Still, if you've already been brave enough to do that, you might have more courage than you think. If not, it's still worth considering, and here's why;

Auditions will be a walk in the park

Getting through a stand-up comedy set will give those bravery muscles a work-out for sure. Getting up there in the first place will be an achievement. Each time you stand in that spotlight, your courage will grow to the point where (hopefully) auditions won't feel nearly as nerve-racking as they used to be. Any negative feedback you get at your auditions could feel mild compared to what has been yelled at you across a darkened bar.

Learning how to improvise

Once you're ready to make that step, you'll find yourself in a quick learning environment. Every audience is different and every location is different too. People in one part of the world might heckle you if they don't like your set, and in another location, you might experience a more awkward silence with an uncomfortable cough. Either situation, and all the ones in between, will require you to turn things around to find that sweet, funny spot or slink off the stage to fight another day

Heckles from the crowd or the sounds of crickets can serve as opportunities to learn how to read the room. It requires a quick wit and improvisation techniques, which can be learned and perfected over time. Improvisation skills can definitely serve you in your acting career. Some fantastic scenes in well-known movies were completely improvised. When interviewed by HitFix, Steve Carell talked about improvising when filming the movie *Anchorman 2*. He shared, 'He (director Andy McKay) really allowed us to try anything. I'd never done anything like that. It was such a great environment because he gave everyone this freedom to fail and try anything.'[14]

Steve Carell Interview

---

14 HitFix. (2013, December 19). *Steve Carell and Paul Rudd discuss hilarious improv moments for 'Anchorman 2'* [Video]. YouTube.

Explore the nuances of comedy

Whether it's from writing and rehearsing your own stuff or listening to other stand-up comedians, you'll soon get to know the subtleties of comedy. There can be a lot of skill involved when it comes to timing, tone and facial reactions. Sometimes, the audience doesn't want to see you laughing at your own jokes; they want to laugh while you remain straight faced. That can be hard to do because laughter is so contagious. But these skills will serve you when interpreting comedy in the scripts that might come your way. There are a hundred different ways to say a line, and you'll be able to show some versatility in your delivery thanks to comedic techniques.

Work while you're between acting gigs

Doing open mic nights between gigs is one way you can keep practising your skills and overcoming those nerves. Who knows, you might even start getting booked to appear, and that would mean receiving some money while you're at it. At any rate, it will be a way for you to keep your performance skills fresh.

Enjoy the comradeship in comedy

Stand-up comedians become a community within themselves. Each knows the rite of passage it takes to become a stand-up comedian, and a sort of support network evolves. Many of the well-known comedic characters in film know each other from the stand-up comedy circuit. The connections you make in this field could help you when a project rolls up that other comedians are involved in.

Crafting your set

You will need to carefully construct your material. There is a level of improvisation, but the core of your set will be pre-written and rehearsed. So, if you're going to take the plunge into stand-up comedy, here are some important factors to consider:

Consistency and change

Some days, you'll hit the mark and you'll be electrified by the laughter of the audience. Other times, even the next night, with a different audience, you could bomb. But for the most part, you will learn what jokes generally land well and what topics make people laugh, groan or squirm. Most comedians use the same material night after night, but change it over time to comment and reflect on the social climate and current events. You'll also use those improv skills to cater your content to the audience, tailoring it as you go. You'll rehearse and perfect your core content, but part of your show will be created on the fly as you engage with your audience, and that engagement is the lifeblood of the show.

Tweak and tweak again

If the audience didn't laugh much tonight, don't throw your jokes out yet. See how they land the next time. But if the audience isn't laughing night after night, then it's likely your material needs adjusting. Perhaps it's your delivery or the joke needs more set-up. It might take only a few small tweaks for the same joke to turn chuckles into roars of laughter. Be willing to take direction from the audience and use that awful silence for your benefit.

Be you or a version of you

Many comedians draw their material from their own personal experiences. It's a great way to introduce yourself as an authentic person with struggles like anyone else. Tig Notaro did the ultimate authentic and exposing stand-up comedy set entitled 'Live', where she talked openly about her cancer diagnosis. It's definitely worth listening to if you want a masterclass on authentic comedy.[15]

Tig Nataro interview

If being fully yourself feels like too much, then you can always do what you do best - act! Some comedians do their set as a character, such as Daniel Whitney, who does his set as Larry the Cable Guy.[16] Others portray a modified version of themselves. In that way, you can feel the protection of the character mask while also basing your material on your personal life experiences.

15 Fox 29 Philadelphia. (2023, July 18). *Comedian and actress Tig Notaro on the legendary 'Hello, Good Evening, I Have Cancer' standup set* [Video]. YouTube.
16 Danica Patrick. (2021, Nov 9). *Daniel Whitney | Larry the Cable Guy | Comedy Gave me Confidence | Clips 01 |* [Video]. YouTube.

Daniel Whitney Interview

This is your chance to take risks and try out new characters. Have you been working on impersonations? See how they land. There's no director and no script except the one you've written. The audience will let you know if you're on or off track (gulp!).

Could you be a comedic writer?

If you're writing material that's hitting the mark, you might have stumbled upon another avenue to acting. Writing for television shows, such as *Saturday Night Live*, late night talk shows or even sitcoms, could bring you closer to the set you long to be on. Tina Fey is an excellent example of an actor who took this path. She started out in an improvisation group and progressed as a writer for *Saturday Night Live*.[17] She became head writer and starred in many of the sketches she wrote. Eventually, she was in a position to pitch her idea for the TV show *30 Rock* to NBC executives, which she also starred in. She also wrote and acted in the films *Mean Girls* and *Baby Mama*. I've said it before: there are many paths to becoming an actor, and writing comedy is one of them.

---

17 Brown, M. (2015, March 27). *Why Tina Fey is a Screenwriting Trailblazer*. The Script Lab.

Consider joining an improv group

If you'd rather have a team comedy experience, you could join your local improv group. Improv is a form of live theatre in which the entire performance is made up on the spot with the help of prompts from either the audience or a host. In parts of the world, it's called 'theatre sports'. Watch episodes of *Whose Line Is It Anyway?* or *Thank God You're Here* to give you an idea of the fun you'll be having. Some improv groups run courses if you'd like to learn those skills in a dedicated way rather than as you go.

A good improv artist will find a way to weave what's currently in the news or circulating on social media into a skit, making it relatable to the audience, so keep up to date on current events and trends. Improv theatre is a great way to keep you on your toes and strengthen your creativity and imagination. I used to be part of a group called the Improv Bandits, and we had a lot of fun performing at a dinner theatre.

Most of the great comedians we see on the big screen today did their share of open mic nights. It's a great way to work out the kinks in your performance if you think you could survive the odd tumbleweed blowing past. Here are some well-known comedic actors that started out doing open-mic nights:

Jamie Foxx
Michael Keaton
Whoopie Goldberg[18]

---

18 Vitale Perez, M. (2022, November 5). *Stand-Up Comedians Who Became Great Actors*. Movieweb.

You might have already decided that stand-up comedy isn't for you, and that's fair. It's not for everyone, and it's best to do it only if you are willing to put yourself out there completely. It's not something to be done half-heartedly. But if you've been looking for something that will challenge you in new ways and take your stage performance to a new level, stand-up comedy might be the thing you're looking for. If you're not ready to join an improv group or give stand-up comedy a try, you could still learn a lot by watching some in action. Just make sure you watch with an intention to learn rather than be entertained (more on this in chapter nine) and clap loudly for every brave comedian who takes the stage.

If you've never performed in front of a live audience before, then starting with stand-up comedy would be akin to diving in the deep end. If you like to put yourself in sink-or-swim situations or enjoy ripping off band aids, then go right ahead. Otherwise, introduce yourself to the stage by doing a few plays with your local theatre group, which we cover in the chapter ahead.

CHAPTER EIGHT

Amateur Theatre

Like stand-up comedians, theatre actors have audiences that give them instant feedback on how they're doing. I was once in a play with a mock sex scene that was supposed to be humorous, but for some audiences, we found the reaction was more shock and horror than giggles and laughter. As cringey as it was to hear a pin drop when there should have been laughter, those missed moments encouraged me to change up my delivery and think on my feet. Despite the fickle nature of audiences, I still maintain that being on stage is an experience like no other. It didn't end up being my career path, but I learned a lot from all the theatre acting I did.

What is amateur theatre?

In a nutshell, when an actor joins an amateur theatre, they will take part in performances where they are not paid for their time. Usually, the actors are not professionally trained, but they might be or have intentions to do that in the future.

A lot of well-known actors started their careers in theatre before jumping over to film, including:

Morgan Freeman
John Goodman
Sarah Jessica Parker
Emma Thompson[19]

Where to start

If you feel excited and inspired to dive into theatre, that's wonderful. There's no time like the present to get started. You will have to do some legwork to begin with, and once you're cast, that's when the hard work begins. But don't get ahead of yourself; start by deciding which amateur theatre you'd like to join.

Do your research

A quick search online should reveal to you where your local amateur theatre clubs are and what's involved to join. There's usually an annual membership fee, but the benefits you'll receive from being part of a theatre community will make it more than worth it, in my opinion. Visit your local theatres, find out who runs them and go to see the plays they put on. Find out when they're holding auditions for their next production, and get yourself there.

Start as soon as you can

If you're still in high school or at university, join the drama club and start gaining theatre experience straight out of the gate. The sooner you take part in the world of drama, the better.

---

19 Brown, S. (2018, August 15). *15 Actors You Didn't Know Had Musical Theater Backgrounds*. Backstage.

Keep an eye on the theatre companies

Once you have a bunch of plays under your belt and you're feeling more confident, get yourself along to the open auditions that theatre companies sometimes hold. Research the play before you audition. Give an authentic and realistic performance by dressing and sounding like the time and place it is set.

Swing actor opportunities

When a big production comes to town, this is your chance to try to get a part as a swing actor. A swing actor often plays a few different smaller roles in a production. When *Jersey Boys* came to my town, I was employed with them as an accent coach. The main character was flown in from New York, but the swing actors were sourced locally, and once they were found, they travelled all over the country as a group.

Rehearsal etiquette

If all your hard work has resulted in you being cast in an amateur theatre production, well done. Now it's time to knuckle down, focus and channel your energy into this role.

Even if theatre acting is not your dream career, it's worth giving it a proper chance because there is so much you can learn from being on stage. At the same time, your heart needs to be in this for it to work. Don't just join a play because you want something to put on your CV or because you're following some sort of '10 steps to being an actor' plan. A production is a team, and every player needs to do their part. You need to be committed to getting to each rehearsal, learning your lines and doing your best performance. If you're not taking it seriously, you will frustrate the cast who want to put on a quality show. When rehearsals begin, ensure you have everything you need and do what's expected of you.

What to wear

During rehearsals, the cast generally wear 'rehearsal blacks'. These are dark-coloured clothing items that are not baggy but let you move freely. Nude-coloured underwear would be good in case you are asked to try on a costume. If you're in a musical, you might need to keep tap or dance shoes in your theatre bag. Sometimes, the costume department will let you wear your costume shoes so you can start moving around in them and building your character's walking style, etc. Some theatres can be a bit draughty. A jumper or jacket you can throw on to keep you warm might be a good idea.

What to bring

Water! Staying hydrated is super important, especially if you're in a musical where you'll be singing and dancing a lot. After all that singing and dancing, you could get sweaty, so bring a hand towel in your theatre bag to wipe yourself off with if you need to. Some body spray and breath mints might also be good. If your theatre company allows it, throw in some snacks you can consume quickly and easily if you feel faint. Bananas are quick and easy, and maybe some nuts. Hopefully, you won't need it, but just in case you do, put your pre-highlighted script with all your notes in your bag as well. Bring a couple of pencils so you can write notes on the script as needed. The notes could change over time, and that's why it's important not to write with a pen. These days, many people keep their scripts on iPads or tablets. Either way, it's handy to have your script to refer to.

Be respectful

Arrive at least ten minutes early to say your hellos, drop your things and be in place on time. Come even earlier if you intend on doing stretches and vocal warmups. Just because you are arriving early doesn't mean you should roll out of bed and head straight to the theatre. Allow yourself enough time to shower so you can turn up fresh and clean. Acting can put you in close proximity to your fellow cast members, and I'm sure they'll be grateful for your effort. Once you arrive, put your phone on silent. Don't be the actor who breaks everyone's concentration with a loud and annoying ringtone echoing throughout the theatre.

The benefits of doing amateur theatre

Even if you're not intending to have a career in theatre, there is a lot to be gained in terms of skills and experience when taking part in a stage performance. I've enjoyed being involved in all sorts of productions from comedies to musicals. I absolutely loved doing them, and in my opinion, there are many great reasons for actors to give amateur theatre a go.

Finding community

A play is a group activity. You will be surrounded by people who, like you, love acting. A play provides an opportunity for you to build bridges and be a supportive part of a production. In a profession riddled with rejection and disappointment, take any chance you can to cheer on your fellow actors; you all need as much support as you can get.

Learn about stage productions

It certainly couldn't hurt for you to learn what you can about lights, props, costumes and all the other aspects that make a stage production great. Knowledge in technical areas can only help.

Lines!

I remember feeling overjoyed when I was cast in a play and then quickly descended into panic when I saw the script and realised the sheer number of lines I would have to memorise. Nothing is more motivating regarding learning your lines than knowing you're going to be standing in front of a live audience. There is a prompter at the front of the stage if the line simply cannot be found in your head, but you want this to be your last resort. Although memorising your lines might feel overwhelming, at the very least, your efforts will help you become a memory master. We cover memorising techniques in chapter eleven, which will hopefully help you feel more confident about your capabilities.

Control over your performance

The director will help you perfect your onstage performance during rehearsals, but when the curtain rises, it will be all on you to bring it home. There won't be anyone calling 'Cut!' or asking you to do it ten more times. It might be a little nerve-racking knowing you have only one chance during each performance to nail the scene, but you will be able to act unimpeded and fully surrender to the flow of the scene.

Crush it

Once you've got a part in a play, push yourself to deliver a memorable performance. There are collectives of theatre professionals who travel from local theatre to local theatre watching and looking for talent to bring over to their theatre company. You never know who is sitting in the audience, so act your heart out every time the curtain rises.

Applause

Applause is scarce when you're filming movies or television, so it's certainly something to appreciate when doing theatre. The cheers, whistles and throwing of flowers is something I could never get sick of.

Let's tackle your stage fright

To act is to be observed. If you love the idea of acting but hate being watched, you're in a real pickle. The first thing to know is that you are not alone. Almost every actor gets nervous at some point, whether they're about to audition, go on stage or see their work up on the big screen. I'm no stranger to nerves, and I still have to navigate them regularly. Here are some suggestions as to how you might calm your nerves:

Your audience is human

There are no perfect people. Remember that the people out there about to watch you are human beings just like you. But instead of trying to degrade your audience by picturing them naked or in their underwear, remember that your wish is to connect with them deeply. Your nerves and vulnerability are part of what builds that bridge between them and you.

Stay fed and watered

My tummy likes to play havoc with me when I'm nervous, which only puts me more on edge. When it's time for me to open my mouth, I want to say my lines, not burp. If nerves tend to make you sweaty or give you digestive issues, you could try soothing your stomach by sipping a herbal tea. If you are prone to nerves, it's best not to eat heavy meals or anything overly fried or fatty before performing. You might crave sugar or caffeine, but they are unlikely to help and could possibly make you feel worse. A light meal or snacks like crackers will help, along with sips of water.

Nerves can make you feel like you need to pee a lot, but don't try and fix that by skipping water. If you had to choose between fainting or needing to pee, I'm sure you'd pick the latter.

Calm your mind

More often than not, the source of your tummy problems is in your brain. Stressful thoughts and feelings can have a biochemical effect on the digestive system; this is known as the gut–brain connection.[20] It's easier said than done to calm your mind when you are about to step on stage, and every person is different. What works for one person may not work for another.

Some people use meditation to clear their minds. There are lots of apps and online recordings of guided meditations that could be helpful to listen to on headphones backstage. Other people use breathing exercises, which can work well because our

20 Diseases & Conditions. *The gut-brain connection* (2023, July 18). Harvard Health Publishing.

body is always here and now. It's never off with your thoughts panicking about all the worst-case scenarios. You can also try clenching your fists and scrunching up your toes really hard so that it's almost painful and then releasing them. This sensation is supposed to help collect your focus to the present moment. Do it three times and then check in with yourself. Hopefully, you will notice that you're feeling calmer.

If none of these suggestions help, I'm sure you will find many more relaxation and confidence-boosting tips for actors online.

Confidence Boost Ted Talk

After auditioning and participating in some plays, you might want to consider deepening your talent with study, professional training or learning new skills. Keeping a thirst for knowledge is an important part of being an actor. Act Two ahead is focused on the theme of learning. Let's dive in and explore the many ways you can build on your acting experience.

ACT TWO

CHAPTER NINE

Watching Movies, Television, and Plays

As a child, I remember curling up on the couch with my mum on rainy Sundays to watch the classics on TV. I especially loved musicals. I wanted to be Elvis' girlfriend and Doris Day's best friend. The singing, the dancing and the costumes all looked like great fun. As I got older, I explored more film genres, from fantasy to gangster films. There were just so many characters, and I wanted to be all of them. I'm sure we can all list films, shows and plays that captured our hearts and imaginations. The ones that made our eyes twinkle and our hearts declare, 'I want to do that!' As actors, it's important we continue to observe and be inspired by acting. There's so much out there to see and so many great actors to learn from.

How will watching acting help you as an actor?

Having a sound knowledge of movies, television shows and plays will help you in your acting journey in many ways. It will deepen your appreciation of acting and also of the incredible amount of work that goes into creating those works of art. Study them as a budding artist might study a painting. Watch the acting carefully, while also looking at all the threads weaving together to create a final piece. Consider the costuming, set design and soundtrack. How do they add to the overall experience?

The acting world is full of film enthusiasts

People who work in films, television and theatre generally have a love of the industry. They share trivia and discuss all sorts of topics, from alternate endings to easter eggs (hidden messages) and metaphorical storylines. If the chance comes, you could join in these conversations with your own views and knowledge. You certainly don't want to be in a situation where you're asked to share your perceptions on, say, a cult classic, having never watched it. Mix up your viewing list to include classics, recent Oscar winners, B-grade horrors, festival films, comedies and musicals. Aim to observe a range of cinematic experiences.

'Must Watch' Movies for Every Actor

Learn about then, and learn about now

It's important that you are aware of what's popular now. If everyone's talking about a particular film or show, watch it and find out why. But don't make the mistake of only viewing recent material. The classics are classics for a reason.

Anyone who writes black-and-white films off as irrelevant and boring has clearly never taken in the cinematic mastery of *Citizen Kane* or *Psycho*. Older movies had to find inventive ways to reach the imagination of their audience. The use of light and shadow in film noir, for example, could create tension and scare an audience silly. Cinematographers of the past used all sorts of inventive tools and techniques to create visual effects, such as smearing Vaseline on the camera lens to give starlets a glowing look.[21] Before the use of modern sound effects, Foley Artists were in common use (named after Jack Foley, who invented the Foley stage and the specific sound-making techniques) and are in fact still used today for sounds that need to be recorded live. There is also a lot of clever camera work and amazing acting on display in classic films.[22] You are missing out if you haven't given them a chance.

Who did it first?

Get curious about your industry by taking a journey back in time. Watch some of the first silent films (which are where it all began). Did you know, for instance, that the 1920 film *The Cabinet of Dr Caligari* was the first to use a twist ending.[23] It's fascinating to learn about the origins of storytelling techniques, the different genres of film and the movies that defined them.

And we're still coming up with new genres, such as 'found footage', which started with *Cannibal Holocaust* in 1980 and

21 Oliver, D. (2015, April 14). *The Vaesline Camera Trick That Gave Old Hollywood Actresses A Gorgeous Glow*. HuffPost.
22 Wolf, D. (2012, February/March). *Jack Foley and the Art of Sound*. Irish America.
23 Evangelista, R. (2023, August 26). *This is the First Movie to Ever Have a Twist Ending*. Collider.

became more famous later with movies such as *The Blair Witch Project* and *Paranormal Activity*. The clever marketing behind *The Blair Witch Project* produced a huge amount of hype that had everyone questioning whether the film was fictional or real.[24] I remember feeling more scared about going to see it than actually watching it.

The TV series *Lost* also played with blurring the lines between reality and fiction by creating real websites for fans to visit for fake companies that featured in the series like the Dharma Initiative and Oceanic Airlines.[25] Fun fact – Oceanic Airlines is a fake airline that has been used in many films and TV shows. [26] It's a company version of the Wilhelm scream, which is another neat industry secret if you want to look it up.

Advancements in cinematic technology, such as the use of green screens and computer-generated imagery (CGI) are also really interesting to research. *Jurassic Park* was the first film to integrate CGI with animatronics in live action scenes.[27] I remember going to see it in a theatre that had new Dolby surround sound technology. My friend and I were blown away. It really felt like dinosaurs were running behind us. The first thing we talked about when we got out of the theatre was when we were going to see it again. Money was tight, but it wasn't a choice. We simply had to buy another ticket.

---

24 Ferguson, M. (2021, October 3). *How the Blair Witch Project Changed Movie Marketing.* Screenrant.

25 Wiki. Websites. Lostpedia Fandom.

26 Oceanic Airlines, TV Tropes

27 Jurassic Park, Industrial Light & Magic.

Watching with a plan

Before you sit down with some popcorn to do some research, remember you are watching to learn and not to enjoy. Don't find yourself swept into the story, forgetting to keenly observe and take notes. This is not movie night with your friends unless your friends are fellow actors and will take watching as seriously as you will.

If you haven't watched a lot of TV, movies or plays, then you have some catching up to do, but don't get overwhelmed. Just set aside some regular viewing time and eventually you'll build a considerable library of titles in your knowledge bank. Make a plan and work through it step by step. Review each movie, TV show and play like you would a textbook, slowly and methodically. So, what do you intend to watch, and what will you look for when you do?

Consider a body of work

You might start off easy by watching all the movies of your favourite actor or director. It would be great to choose someone who has played all kinds of roles or directed movies from different genres.

When looking at an actor's body of work, you might notice how their skills developed over time. Perhaps their earlier work had less depth, or perhaps they've always been great. It's also interesting to see what films gave well-known actors their start. How many started out in cheesy horrors or teen flicks? How many were cast in a low-budget film that just happened to be a blockbuster hit?

Pause at crucial scenes

Take notes on how the scene was conveyed. As you move through the scene, note the different camera angles that were used. Is there continuity between the shots? Are their hand movements consistent? Have props been moved? Consider all the components of the scene, such as lighting and sound. How do they add to the general effect?

Consider the realism aspect

Some scenes look so real because they are. For example, watch the famous 'falling scene' in the breakout movie *Die Hard*. Actor Alan Rickman wasn't truly dangling out the window of a high-rise building, but he was being suspended forty feet in the air with an airbag below. The plan was to release the cord suspending him and capture his facial expression as he dropped. A countdown was being yelled out to prepare him for the fall, but the crew were instructed to release him early. The result is what you see in the movie. A perfect slow-motion shot of his face truly turning to terror before falling to his imaginary death.[28]

Alan Rickman's Famous Fall

---

28 OSSA Movies. (2022, January 5). *Die Hard Without Stunts and Effects | OSSA Movies* [Video]. YouTube.

There are lots of ways that actors create real experiences in fake environments. Kirsten Dunst, for example, received an Oscar nomination for her role in Jane Campion's *Power of the Dog*. She shared in an interview with the AV Club that she would spin in circles before the camera started rolling to accurately portray a drunk woman. She didn't need to be drunk to do a convincing performance; she just needed to authentically feel the dizziness and nausea that can be experienced by an intoxicated person.[29]

Kirsten Dunst Interview

Trying to elicit an authentic response from an actor doesn't always work the way a director intends. On a particular film I was cast in, the director told me to open a door and react to what I saw without being told what I would find. I opened the door and discovered an actor covered in blood on the other side. I promptly threw my character's accent out the window and called out loudly for an ambulance in my normal talking voice. It wasn't what the director was hoping for, but we are all human, and I was as shocked as I'm sure Alan Rickman was when he found himself falling without warning.

---

29 The A.V. Club. (2021, December 1). *Kirsten Dunst and Jesse Plemons Interview: The Power of the Dog* [Video]. YouTube.

Watch the commentary

Have a look for recorded interviews with actors about the films they've done. Often, they are asked to talk about what it was like to perform a particular scene. You might be surprised to learn what the experience was truly like, and they sometimes share, as Kirsten Dunst did, a tip on how they were able to deliver an authentic performance. Director commentaries are also insightful. They're often added as a bonus feature on DVDs, or sometimes, a 'behind the scenes' documentary is released as a separate film. Jane Campion did a 'behind the scenes' commentary on the *Power of the Dog* for Netflix where she shares the depth she went to in order to bring the characters in the film to life.

Turn the sound off

Go back over scenes you found incredibly powerful in terms of delivery. Turn off the sound and watch closely how the actor embodies the character. Note facial expressions, body movements and how they interact with their environment. There are so many mechanisms that actors use to convey meaning, both obvious and subtle. You might be surprised by how much more you notice when sound effects, music and dialogue are removed. When the sound is off, can you still feel the intensity of the scene?

Read the script

Download the scripts of the movies and TV shows you're watching from sites like Script-O-Rama (www.script-o-rama.com)or the Internet Movie Screenplay Database (IMDb). Compare each scene to what was written.

Did they stay close to the screenplay, or did they modify it? How would you have approached the same scene? As you review script after script, you may notice patterns in how stories are written, a sort of winning formula. If you're interested in the art of storytelling, look up Joseph Campbell's work on *The Hero's Journey*. He puts forward the notion that, generally, all stories follow the same trajectory, starting with a call to adventure.[30] You could also read about the seven basic plots according to author Christopher Booker (2004):

1. Overcoming the Monster
2. Rags to Riches
3. The Quest
4. Voyage and Return
5. Rebirth
6. Comedy
7. Tragedy[31]

Tackling TV shows

There are a lot of TV series out there that are considered by many to be 'must watch' material, from *The Sopranos* to *The Office* and *The Twilight Zone*. You might have watched a lot of television, but we all have a list of TV shows we haven't watched yet that everyone says are amazing. Before you sit down to binge watch all five seasons of *Breaking Bad*, you might want to take a more strategic approach. The first season of a series is not always the best place to start when you are watching to learn. By the second or third season, the actors have truly settled into their characters and perfected their dynamic. The storyline might be harder to

---

30 Joseph Campbell (1949) The Hero With a Thousand Faces. Princeton NJ: Princeton University Press.
31 Christopher Booker (2004) The Seven Basic Plots: Why We Tell Stories. London: Continuum.

follow if you have skipped the first couple of seasons, and therefore lost background information and context. However, you can always go back and watch the beginning seasons at another time when you are watching for enjoyment.

Head to the theatre

Don't forget theatre! Ensure you're getting along to plays regularly too. Again, watch a range of productions from *Hamlet* to *Wicked*. Even if you don't intend on pursuing stage acting as a career, you are likely to do some theatre as part of your acting journey. The people you work with are likely to have some stage experience and a knowledge of theatre productions too. You want to know what someone's talking about when they use a quote from a famous play and join in discussions about theatre and stage acting when they happen around you. So, take an interest in theatre, and go along to plays to gain an appreciation of them. Remember, there is a crossover between different acting mediums. Stage shows can be turned into movies, such as *Les Misérables*, and there are also musical TV shows, like *Glee*.

Like with movies and television, watch plays to learn and not be swept into the experience like a passive audience member. Go prepared by reading the play beforehand. You might even like to do some research on the playwright. What other plays have they written? Where did they draw their inspiration from? How did the director of the play interpret the work? Did they change the setting, perhaps, or the era?

You might not have the budget to buy tickets to big productions when they come to town, but that shouldn't stop you from taking in theatre. Go to local theatres or university productions if you must. You might stumble across some absolutely amazing acting, or you might have to sit through some dismal performances. Either way, take your pen and notebook and write down your observations. Good or bad, you can learn either way.

Observing acting is a great way to deepen your understanding and appreciation of the craft. These are actors who are where you want to be, so take every opportunity you can to gain insights and tips into their methods and experiences. When you're ready to get more physical in your learning, you could take steps towards learning some special skills, but which ones should you learn? Let's discuss.

CHAPTER TEN

Develop Special Skills

Actors are asked to play people from all walks of life, and people from all walks of life have all sorts of special skills. Sometimes, actors are expected to learn special skills as part of their role, and at other times, casting is looking for someone who already has them. It can come down to a number of factors, including time constraints, budget allowances, and sometimes, the look of the actor (especially if they are portraying a real person). Either way, an actor needs to have a willingness to learn new skills to increase their chances of landing roles.

For me personally, I've explored many forms of dance, including ballet, tap and modern jazz. I'm also no stranger to musical instruments. I've learned how to play the clarinet, flute, piano, guitar, recorder and the drums. I really enjoy learning a new instrument, and I find that once you've learned how to play one, the skills you learn can help you more easily pick up another.

What is a special skill?

A special skill is something you have mastered and not something you just dabble in. Being able to say 'Hello' and 'Goodbye' in another language is not enough to put it on your special skills list. Only include skills that took time and dedication to learn.

Your curriculum vitae (CV)

Special skills are generally listed at the bottom of your CV. Be specific about aspects of your skills and how advanced you are. For example, what range do you sing in (alto, baritone, etc.) and what belt level are you at in karate?

I recommend either taking the time to learn how to put together an appealing CV or paying someone to help you do it. Keep in mind that agents are extremely busy people. If they stop to look at your CV, it will be a glance at the most.

CV Templates

Here are the most common headings for an actor's CV:

- Contact Information
- Vitals (height, eye colour, weight, age range)
- Credits - Feature Films
- Credits – Television
- Credits – Theatre

- Training
- Special Skills

If you haven't got any credits yet, include the plays you've taken part in and what training you've done or are currently completing.

Just because special skills are generally listed at the bottom of your CV doesn't mean they're not important. They could be what the casting director looks for first if the skill is crucial to the plot of the story. They may only skim the list or only look at the first one, so make sure you start your list with your most impressive skill. You need to make this section of your CV count and not fill it with irrelevant information, such as 'I'm a bookworm who loves to travel'. You could use it to show special interests, though, which could serve as conversation starters, such as cosplay or LARP (live action role play).

The benefits of learning special skills

You never know what skills the character you will play might need. From skiing to horse riding, almost every special skill under the sun has probably featured in a movie or television show at some point. Ahead, I'll cover what the most sought-after special skills are and how learning them can help you grow as an actor. It's important that I add here that the benefit of learning new skills goes beyond the advancement of your career.

Our passions are part of what make us unique, and pursuing them brings us a level of joy and satisfaction. Not only that, learning a new skill is a great way to meet people, to get off your couch and dive into something intriguing. That the skill you choose to master could also help you land acting roles will be the icing on the cake.

Learning should be a lifelong passion, and I mean for everyone, not just actors. It keeps us from becoming stagnant and falling into the false belief that we have already learned all we need to know.

If you already have some special skills in your cannon, then good for you! No doubt they would tell us something about you, like whether you're artistic or a thrill seeker, for example. That you've become advanced at a particular skill demonstrates your ability to apply yourself and master something new.

If you haven't learned a special skill yet, don't worry or allow yourself to become overwhelmed by the options. Just get curious and see if something sounds interesting or looks like it might be fun.

What special skills are recommended for actors?

In no particular order, the most commonly searched for skills are:

- Accents
- Stand-up or improv
- Musical instruments
- Dancing
- Singing
- Foreign languages
- Stage combat

The first two special skills (accents and stand-up) are covered in more depth in their own chapters in this book. I'll address the other skills shortly, but first I must caution you against being led by a 'must have' list. This could result in you trying to master a skill you actually have no personal interest in or hate doing. You are better to think first about the kind of acting you want to do (stage vs film, for example) and also what kind of characters you'd like to play. Improv skills, for instance, would be a good direction for you to go in if you have an interest in comedic roles. Singing and dance lessons could serve you well if you are interested in theatre. So, with that in mind, let's zoom in on a few particular skills and how they can help you grow as an actor.

Learning an instrument

If an audition has called for actors who know how to play a particular instrument, you may be asked to demonstrate your skills, so don't list it if you are rusty, haven't picked it up in years and actually only know how to play chopsticks on the piano. To master an instrument, I recommend taking lessons from a teacher or following an online course.

Who knows, you might pick it up really quickly, but for most of us, it's understood that becoming proficient at a musical instrument takes dedication and commitment. It could absolutely be worth the time and effort. According to a study at the University of Alberta, learning an instrument can improve your memory, which is crucial for actors.[32] It may be tedious at first, and that's why it's important to choose an instrument that intrigues you, so you actually enjoy learning how to play it.

Instruments can vary widely in price depending on which one you choose. You might find one second hand (in which case you may need to get it professionally tuned), and there are free teaching resources online that could help you get started. You'll have to be doubly committed to be self-taught.

---

32 Gagnon, R., & Nicoladis, E. (2021). Musicians show greater cross-modal integration, intermodal integration, and specialization in working memory than non-musicians. Psychology of Music, 49(4), 718-734. https://doi.org/10.1177/0305735619896088

If you already know how to play an instrument, you're in a good position. If it's been a while since you played, take the time to get your skills back up to scratch. It's worth perfecting your current skills, because it is much harder to learn a completely new instrument.

If you're choosing your first musical instrument, then you have quite a decision to make, but don't worry about picking the 'right' instrument for the business. You are best to choose one that really speaks to you or looks fun.

Singing

Your voice is your first musical instrument. You don't have to buy it from a store, and you can start playing with it as soon as you're ready. It's already there, waiting to be used, so why not give it a try?

If you have been thinking that singing is only for theatrical actors, you're mistaken. Learning to sing provides a lot of benefits for actors. For example, singing will help you become more aware of your breathing, ensuring you take breaths at the right spots as you sing. This can help with delivering your lines. Sometimes, actors are so focused on getting out the words they forget to breathe and their voice becomes strained. Your character isn't thinking about when to breathe as they're speaking because they're not saying lines, they're just talking.

Singing lessons are an expense, but it's difficult to hear yourself as others do. That you sound great in the shower is not going to be enough for auditions. It's important to work with someone who understands pitch and tone. Singing instructors also know when you are using your vocal cords correctly and when you're overdoing it. They'll teach you vocal warm-ups and how to soothe and take care of your throat. Actors sometimes have to do scenes where they shout, cry, scream or laugh over and over. Knowing how to take care of your vocal cords will help you avoid losing your voice, which could push back production.

If you are going to a theatre audition, it's likely they will provide you with a song or two to sing. I suggest you have a few songs you've perfected up your sleeve in case they want to hear something else from you. Just make sure you choose songs you know well that show off your vocal abilities.

At the end of the day, actors are artists and they express the emotion and intention of their character in many ways. Singing is just one of many dramatic tools characters use to convey meaning. If you have no budget for lessons, I suggest you look for a local choir to join; that will give you an environment to practise in regularly, and hopefully you'll get some feedback from the conductor.

Dancing

Dance is an important skill for an actor because it helps you to become acutely aware of your body and how it moves. After all, acting isn't just about delivering lines; you are not a talking head. You will embody a persona who walks a certain way, makes gestures when they talk and expresses themselves with their body just as much as they do with their voice.

If you are drawn to stage acting, then you may require a greater level of skill when it comes to dance or expressive movement, but dance is not only important to theatre actors. All actors would do well to learn dance, if nothing else but for the strength, flexibility and agility it brings to your movement

Dance also helps to loosen the body and shake away stiffness. Even if you never end up dancing in front of a camera, you can use it to stay supple and as a means of de-stressing.

Like learning an instrument, learning choreography is also good for the memory. At a group lesson, you will learn to become in sync with other people in your environment and listen carefully to instructions. Like singing, dance is another way actors convey meaning. It's an expressive tool, and if you let yourself go, it can be an absolute joy. There are beginner classes for every type of dance there is, so don't let your lack of experience hold you back. Dance can be raw and exposing but also exhilarating if you can get past worrying about whether you look silly. Grab some friends if you need support, and have fun.

Learning a language

This is a skill that can serve you both personally and professionally. Deciding to become fluent in another language can be very beneficial as you travel the world and meet new people. You might be surprised at how often it comes in handy.

Depending on which language you choose to learn, it could help you with perfecting an accent. When you become familiar with the distinct sounds of a language, like French, for example, you will understand how those distinct sounds influence the way a French person would speak English. You will be able to authentically speak English with a French accent rather than trying to mimic the sounds. Additionally, learning a language can increase job prospects and allow you to communicate with a greater number of people.

Stage Combat

Otherwise known as fight choreography, stage combat is specialised training that allows actors to safely act out fight scenes. Actors rehearse a fight scene over and over again so the strikes and blows are perfectly timed to allow their scene partner to effectively dodge their punches or create the illusion that they landed. On-set combat choreographers are called fight directors, and they have all sorts of tricks up their sleeves to create believable acts of violence that do zero harm to the actor.

Teaching actors how to do stage combat takes time, and as you know, time is money in this business. If you already have a good handle on basic stage combat techniques, then you're in a good place to hit the ground running in a role that requires these skills.

Stage fighting is another form of expression for you as an actor. It allows you to ground even more deeply into your character, whom, for whatever reason, has resorted to violence. It is a skill taken very seriously by fight directors. That you did one fight scene on a previous production will not be enough to include it in your special skills list. Overstating your skill level and knowledge in this area could put you or your scene partner at risk, so be sure about your level of proficiency before you write it down.

Don't lie

If you have been cast because you have a particular special skill and then don't deliver on it, you will be very unpopular. Don't bank on being able to learn it before you start filming, especially if it's something that takes a long time to master, such as playing an instrument or learning another language. It could also land you in dangerous situations if you said, for example, you're an experienced horse rider and end up breaking your arm when you fall off trying to get on the horse.

If an accent is quite important to casting, you may be asked on the spot to deliver lines in the accent you listed on your CV. I have been in situations where I've been asked to repeat a line in an American accent, and because I know that accent inside out, I can switch to it quickly. You need to be able to do the same. They're not going to like hearing, 'Oh, I can do that accent. I just need to practise'. Everyone can do an accent if they practise; you list it on your special skills because you've already mastered it.

When it comes to special skills in general, that you took a lesson once or did it in high school ten years ago is not enough to include it. Having to recast because an actor lied on their CV is less than ideal. Don't be that person.

Be ready and willing to learn

Productions don't expect their actors to be excellent at everything, so they provide training for a lot of things. Mandy Patinkin is known around the world as the actor who played swordsman Inigo Montoya in the movie *The Princess Bride*, but did you know that he trained with an Olympic fencing coach, Henry Harutunian, and then Olympian fencer Bob Anderson for months to create what is arguably one of the best sword fighting scenes in cinema?[33]

---

33 60 Minutes. (2014, November 17). *Sword Fighting stories from "The Princess Bride"* [Video]. YouTube.

Mandy Patinkin Interview

You don't have to be in a leading role to receive some special skills training. My agency was involved with sourcing extras for the *Lord of the Rings*, *Spartacus* and *Mulan* movies when they were being filmed in New Zealand. Both the extras and the actors cast were sent to boot camp to learn all sorts of skills, from horse riding to sword fighting.

Sometimes, body doubles or special effects can be used to plug the holes in an actor's skills set. Margot Robbie practised ice skating four hours a day, five days a week, for five months, and also had the help of a special effects team to create a convincing portrayal of Tonya Harding in her movie, *I, Tonya*.[34]

I, Tonya video

---

34 Vudu. (2018, April 5) *I, Tonya Behind the Scenes – Creating the VFX (2018)* | *Movieclips Extras* [Video]. YouTube.

Natalie Portman threw herself into her role as a ballerina in *Black Swan*. She trained five hours a day, six days a week, for a year.[35] I imagine neither woman knew just what they could achieve with intensive training, but they were willing to do it to find out.

Natalie Portman's Training for *Black Swan*

Whatever skill you choose to learn, it will take time and dedication. I recommend choosing a few skills to pursue and really mastering them. Being mediocre at lots of things won't help you as much as being highly proficient at particular skills. Stay open to opportunities to learn, and leap at those chances when they come. And don't forget, quite a few of the above skills have the added bonus of strengthening memory skills, which will come in handy when you're memorising lines.

35 SearchlightPictures. (2011, Feb 15) *BLACK SWAN, Featurette: Natalie Portman's Training.* [Video]. YouTube.

CHAPTER ELEVEN

Strengthen Your Memory

When memorising lines, I like to record them on my phone, and then listen to them 24/7 so they really sink in. This is an auditory method of learning, and each of us generally has one method we tend to gravitate towards.

Which one of the four learning styles below appeals to you?

- Visual (using diagrams, graphs, symbols)
- Auditory (listening to others speaking or to your own voice)
- Reading and writing (note taking and reading text)
- Kinaesthetic (hands-on learning, people who learn by doing)[36]

Think back to when you had to memorise the times tables at school. No doubt your teacher used multiple methods to help you remember them. These might have included writing them down repeatedly, saying them out loud again and again, singing them in a song or maybe they used flashcards? If you're like me, you might remember this being a mundane and boring part of school, but memorising your times tables was one of those tasks that truly helped you later in life. On any given day, we come

---

36 Understanding Your Learning Style (2008) Wilfrid Laurier University.

across situations where we have to multiply numbers in our head. If you can do that with relative ease, it's probably thanks to the rote learning you did at school. Do you remember which method suited you best? If not, you can just try different techniques and see which one sticks. You don't have to choose only one; you might combine a few.

Techniques

If you find that no matter how hard you study, you can't seem to recall information later when you need it, then you may not yet have come across a technique that works for you. Not to worry, I've listed some common memory tips below, and I'm sure that one of them will help.

Break it down

If you have a lot of lines to learn, then you probably have landed a significant role. Congratulations! It's easy to get overwhelmed when looking at all your scenes and lines, but you don't have to memorise them all at once. Break them down into manageable chunks.

You might go scene by scene or break them down even further and go line by line. You want to build the script in your memory with each line acting like a building block. Think of it like listening to a new hit song on the radio. At first, you'll pick up a few lyrics as you sing along, but as the station plays the song more frequently, you'll start picking up more lyrics each time you hear it.

Don't worry about how you'll perform as you say the lines yet. Just learn the words, and once you've got them all in your memory, then you can play around with intonation and word emphasis.

Write it down

If something is important to remember, we usually write it down. Sometimes, we use notes as visual reminders, such as a post-it we stick on the refrigerator. But many don't realise that the act of writing itself helps us to remember things. A study completed by the Developmental Neuroscience Laboratory at the Norwegian University of Science concluded that handwriting notes allows for greater memory recall.[37] Essentially, the results of the study found that when you write something down, you use multiple areas of the brain. This allows the information being processed to be encoded more deeply in your memory.

Think about it this way: if you write a grocery list and then forget to take it with you, you'll remember what to buy better than if you hadn't written a list at all and just tried to remember what you saw in the cupboards. For this to work, you have to handwrite the information. Typing it won't have the same effect. Don't worry about your messy handwriting. It's the act of forming words on paper with your hand that assists the memory.

Talk to yourself

Reading your lines out loud to yourself is another technique that uses multiple cognitive processes. You are reading, speaking and listening all at the same time. Try walking in circles while reading your lines out loud to add an additional process to the mix. I suggest finding a private location to do this so the

---

37 Ose Askvik Eva, van der Weel F. R. (Ruud), van der Meer Audrey L. H. The Importance of Cursive Handwriting Over Typewriting for Learning in the Classroom: A High-Density EEG Study of 12-Year-Old Children and Young Adults. *Frontiers in Psychology* 11, (2020). https://doi.org/10.3389/fpsyg.2020.01810

police don't get calls about a person walking in circles talking to themselves. When you're ready, gather a small audience of friends or family. You don't want the audition or day one on set to be the first time you say these lines in front of other people. Watch out for nerves and stage fright, which can quickly undo all your memory work. I've certainly had that terrible experience of walking into an audition, only to find that the lines I memorised had done a disappearing act. Look back at chapter eight – 'Amateur Theatre' for tips on managing your nerves.

Test yourself

Are you a flash card kind of person? Write your scene partner's lines on cards and see if you can remember what you're supposed to say in response. Or maybe write your own lines on them and see if you can remember what your next line is. Again, it all comes down to learning styles and what works for you. Instead of flash cards, you could get some colourful sticky notes and post them around your home. Stick them on the outside of your shower or on the back of the toilet door. When I have an audition coming up, my script is in my hand from the moment I wake up until I fall asleep at night. I always have it with me so I can look at my lines in every spare moment.

Listen to a recording

If you've been driven out of your home or flat because the people who live with you are sick of hearing you rehearse, then take a break, put on some headphones and listen to a recording of yourself instead. Listen to your lines on repeat as you walk the dog, get the groceries or run on the treadmill. Trying to recall your lines while simultaneously doing something else, like exercising or washing the dishes, strengthens your memory even further. It helps you access your memory while being in a potentially distracting environment, and let's face it, sets and stages are busy places.

Sing it!

How did you learn your ABCs? Depending on where you live, you might have sung the alphabet song in the tune of 'Twinkle, twinkle, little star' like a lot of pre-schoolers. It's no accident that this technique was used. Several studies have been published on music and memory, including one by the University of Edinburgh, which looked specifically at using music to help participants remember a foreign language.[38] Three groups were taught Hungarian words. One group learned by speaking the words, another group spoke the words with a beat rhythm and the third group sung them. After fifteen minutes, they were tested, and the singing group had the best recall of the lot. You could dive deep into the scientific findings on the neurology of the brain, but in summary, they have found that the brain is more receptive to new information when it enters via a catchy or memorable tune.

Think about it. Have you ever been listening to the radio and been surprised that you can remember every word of a song that you loved but hadn't heard in years? I know I have. Singing is a powerful memory mechanism if you're keen to try it. Just remember, you will need to switch from singing to speaking once you have the lines memorised.

---

38 Ludke, K.M., Ferreira, F. & Overy, K. Singing can facilitate foreign language learning. *Mem Cogn* 42, 41–52 (2014). https://doi.org/10.3758/s13421-013-0342-5

Run lines with a partner

Most of the time, if you're saying lines, it's because someone else is in the scene with you, so you'll need a reader. I personally like to highlight my lines in the script first, then I record them and listen to them before bringing in a reader.

To ensure you've got the lines etched in your memory, you can do an 'Italian run' with your partner. An Italian run is when you say the lines with your reader as quickly as possible. Each time you pause to remember or stumble as you try to recall the words reveals where your weak spots are in your memory.

Running lines with a fellow actor will allow you to have in-depth discussions about the scene and how you want to play it. Together, you can get into the purpose of the scene. Discuss the emotion behind each line and why it's said. For me, when I start saying the lines with another person, that's when I begin connecting more deeply with the story and expressing the lines with greater authenticity. I'm no longer saying the lines to an imaginary person while I'm driving my car; I'm in a real person-to-person environment.

Your reader may use a tone or delivery style you hadn't expected. There was an occasion where I couldn't get my head around a particular line in a script I was working on. No matter how I read it, it made no sense. It wasn't until my reading partner said his line out loud that I realised my line was supposed to be read in a sarcastic tone. Suddenly, it made sense, and I could see how the line added to the scene. That's why running lines is so helpful, because the delivery won't be written in the script. The casting director won't tell you how to say the audition lines; they want to see how you interpret them.

Use an app

If you can't find a single soul to read lines with, there are a number of apps that can serve as electronic readers, such as Rehearsal Pro. You can record your scene partner's lines onto the app and then run through scenes again and again. On the upside, an app is available to run lines with you at any time and will never get tired or bored of rehearsing with you, but it will never replace working with a real live human being. It's just the next best thing.

Sleep on it

Putting your script under your pillow each night won't help you remember it, but ensuring you get at least seven hours of sleep each night definitely will. Numerous studies confirm the benefits of sleep regarding memory, such as the one undertaken by KT Potkin & WE Bunney on the effect of sleep on long-term memory in early adolescence.[39] Their research found that new information absorbed by the brain when awake is transferred to long-term memory storage during specific phases of sleep.

Interestingly, it's not enough to learn and then go to sleep for everything to sink in. When you wake up, you need to actively recall the information you learned before sleeping to build a neurological pathway back to wherever your brain has stored it. So, memorise, sleep, recall, then repeat to keep accessing those lines. Sleeping not too long after learning further assists with transferring information into long-term memory, so unless you

39 Potkin KT, Bunney WE Jr (2012) Sleep Improves Memory: The Effect of Sleep on Long Term Memory in Early Adolescence. PLoS ONE 7(8): e42191. https://doi.org/10.1371/journal.pone.0042191

like the idea of studying just before bed, perhaps schedule a nap between memorising sessions.

Cram...sometimes

Cramming only helps you to remember information for a short period of time. That's why students will often engage in an intense period of study a few hours before a test. They'll walk in with the information fresh in their minds. So, if you've got a scene to film, find a quiet spot and cram those lines in your head. After a scene is finished, the lines can drop out of your head, and you can start cramming for the next scene. But if you're in a theatre production, cramming will not help you one bit. You need to remember your lines for all your scenes (not a scene at a time), and you need to remember them day after day until your production is finished. So, a last-minute cram can help, but only in some situations, and since you will find yourself in all kinds of roles and various types of production, you'll want to develop a variety of memorising techniques. You'll know once your lines have been embedded in your memory properly because you will feel no fear about whether you will recall the lines when you need them. That's when you'll know that you've learned those lines inside out, upside down and backwards.

Play with your deliveries

Casting directors are sometimes looking to see who took an interesting take on the scene, so don't be afraid to try different angles. Say a line ten different ways, even if it's just to confirm how you're NOT going to say it. Doing this will help you remain open to direction when it comes time to perform. If you've been rehearsing saying the lines in only one way, you might find it hard to change it up if asked. For many, it's harder to forget something you've memorised than to absorb something new. I once had a student who was preparing for an upcoming audition and I was teaching them a particular accent. We ran into real problems because they had memorised the lines using a stern tone of delivery when it was meant to be comedic, and on top of that, they had memorised the line incorrectly. I had my work cut out to help them change their tone, accent and words in time for their audition. That's why it's crucial to memorise the lines (correctly) first, then layer the accent on top and try different delivery styles last.

Mind the gap

There's this thing actors do when they've forgotten their lines, and it drives me nuts. They take a deep breath in, pause, and then let it out in a kind of sigh. It gives them just enough time to scramble inside their heads and pull the lines out of their memory banks. I've used it myself when I've been running around inside my mind screaming, 'Oh my god, oh my god, where's the line?' and the casting director will tell me we need to go again because I took a weird breath.

Of course, after doing a scene for what feels like the billionth time, you'll do anything to convince the casting director that it was on purpose. However, most of the time, there's no reason at all for your character to stop and sigh. It's a random pause that doesn't make sense and totally breaks the scene. And even if you think nobody noticed, I can assure you the casting director did, and they knew you were thinking about your lines.

A strong memory allows you to bring forward an amazing performance. Think of it like a singer. They can't show us the range of their vocals, the emotion of a song or even the melody if they start making mumbling noises into the mic because they don't know the words. When your lines are properly memorised, your dialogue can become an authentic expression of your character rather than something you're reciting from memory. That's when you can start playing with a scene, and a monologue is a good place to start.

CHAPTER TWELVE

Memorise Monologues

Now that you've explored different techniques for memorising lines, you can put them to good use learning some monologues. You don't need another actor (usually) to act out a monologue, so you can play with them at home and try all kinds of deliveries. I collect monologue scripts and put them all over my house. Next to mirrors, on the backs of doors, on the kitchen bench, anywhere I can spend some time glancing at them again and again.

But which monologues should you memorise? I'll cover how to choose a good audition monologue shortly, but before I do, let's look at the basics first. What is a monologue? And what is its purpose?

What is a monologue?

The word 'monologue' originates from the Greek words *monos* (one/alone) and *logos* (speech). In other words, it's a speech spoken by one person alone. That doesn't necessarily mean that the person is alone in the scene (although they may be); it specifically means they will speak for a length of time uninterrupted.

What is the purpose of a monologue?

You might already have a good understanding of what monologues are and how they're used within scripts. If not, your first task should be familiarising yourself with them and gaining an appreciation of their purpose.

If you've read chapter nine, you'll already know how important it is to study a wide range of plays, movies and television shows. As part of your viewing plan, you might like to note the monologues you come across. Write down how they were used to add to the story and what you noticed about the actor's delivery.

The writer of the script didn't just think, 'Hmmm, maybe I'll just put a monologue here'. They wanted the monologue to enrich the viewer's experience. For example, it might have been used to help the audience gain a better understanding of a character and how they relate to the larger story being told. Watch the monologue told by Captain Quint (played by Robert Shaw) in the cult classic *Jaws*.[40] Listening to his chilling monologue tells you all you need to know about why his character joined a hunting expedition for a man-eating shark. Interesting fact: the story he shares about the sinking of the USS Indianapolis is based on a true event.[41]

---

40 Movieclips. (2011, May 28). *Jaws (1975) – The Indianapolis Speech Scene (7/10) | Movieclips* [Video]. YouTube.
41 Davidson, L. (2023, May 9). *The Deadly Sinking of the USS Indianapolis.* History Hit.

Sarah Valentine

Jaws Monologue

Some suggest reading the entire script or play to give you context. Or you could watch the film or television series if you're a more visual person. Ultimately, what you want to know is what the events were that led to the monologue being said and what happened as a consequence of it being spoken.

Be prepared

If you've managed to score a meeting with an agent, you might be asked to perform a monologue. Hopefully, you'll get some notice if that's the case, but either way, go prepared. Before an actor would meet with me at my agency, I would send them a couple of scenes to practise, and I'd ask them to prepare a monologue of their choice. That left the ball in their court to cast themselves in a role they'd love to land.

You are unlikely to be asked to do a monologue at an audition for a film or television show. However, it does happen on rare occasions. During the four years I worked as a casting director, I think there were only two times where I asked an actor to show me something extra. One of the actors had nothing prepared so, unfortunately, I couldn't progress with them. It was such a shame because I really thought this actor had some chops, but they didn't quite have the lines down. If they'd had a monologue ready to go, I think they would have had a good shot. The other actor I asked actually had a monologue prepared, but it was from a Shakespearean play. That would have been great if I was casting for a play, but I wasn't. It wasn't appropriate, and it didn't help me imagine them in this particular role. So, although I commend them for having a monologue memorised, it is important to think about the character you're auditioning for when selecting a monologue. An actor needs to be prepared for anything.

Monologues in theatre

Most drama schools hold auditions when selecting students for their programmes. Audition requirements vary, but almost all will require the student to perform at least two contrasting monologues to show their range. For example, you might choose a classic and a contemporary monologue or a dramatic and a comedic monologue. They will expect theatrical monologues, so choose them from plays rather than from movies or television shows. Some drama schools give each actor a chance to deliver a monologue for visiting agents as part of their end-of-year showcase.

When auditioning for a part in a play, not only should you choose a monologue that plays to your strengths, you want the monologue to be a fit for the character you're auditioning for.

Choosing an audition monologue

Monologues were not written with auditions in mind. The screenplay writer was, as I said before, thinking about the best way to tell the story. Resist the temptation to type into an Internet search engine 'best monologues of all time' to point you in the direction of your audition monologue. Of course, it's wonderful to be inspired by the many amazing monologues that have been delivered on stage and on screen, but choosing a monologue to showcase your abilities should not start with an Internet search. It starts with an awareness and understanding of the character you're auditioning for or of the character you would most like to portray.

If you've been asked to choose a monologue to showcase yourself, you need to stop and think about what your dream role would be. You know yourself better than anyone else, so you know what role would be perfect for you. Find that character in a play, show or film, and practise one of their monologues.

When you have a few practised and perfected monologues tucked away in your mind, you can walk into any audition space knowing you have an ace up your sleeve. Even if you end up never needing them, they're there to give you a confidence boost.

Not all monologues are an ideal choice for auditions. There are some specific features you should look for when selecting audition monologues or for impressing an agent:

It isn't too long

We live in a fast-paced world, no one has any time and our attention spans are getting shorter by the day. Most recommend that an audition monologue be no longer than ninety seconds, but truth be told, they have probably made up their minds ten seconds in. If they like what they see in the first ten seconds, everything you do after could potentially change their mind, so keep it short.

I could always tell pretty quickly if an actor's monologue was going downhill. I want someone to grasp my attention from the first line. Think of yourself as a fisherman looking to hook your audience from the start. Be wary of monologues that build too slowly or have a powerful end sentence because you might not even get the chance to say it. Think of how many times judges on the TV talent shows hit their X buttons if someone starts off poorly. They might have had a really impressive finale, but you can't take the judges' time and attention for granted.

Don't assume they'll let you finish. They may have many people to see, so someone may literally be keeping time. Start with an intention to wow them straight away because you may not have the time to redeem yourself otherwise. Practise at home with a stopwatch and try to come under your time limit so you have some breathing room on the day.

It has emotional range

The opening monologue said by the character Patrick Bateman in *American Psycho* is well known, but it is essentially delivered in a monotone voice.[42] That's because the character is a sociopath, and it's appropriate for him to talk that way. The purpose of his monologue is to introduce himself as the main character. This relates to what I was saying before about looking up famous monologues. Just because it is famous or well-known does not make it a good audition choice. An appropriate audition monologue takes the audience on an emotional journey. There doesn't have to be a lot of different emotions, just more than one. Some people think a highly emotional monologue is best, but that's not necessarily the case. You don't want to choose a monologue because the character is yelling with rage or

42 Movieclips. (2012, March 16). *Morning Routine – American Psycho (1/12) Movie CLIP (2000) HD* [Video]. YouTube.

hysterically crying through the whole thing. It's no different from using Patrick Bateman. You are not showing any range. If the monologue starts with intense emotions, it has nowhere to build to. You might choose something that starts off calm and ends in rage, or you might start off in laughter and end in deep sadness.

Patrick Bateman's Monologue

I'll also add here that unless you have mastered crying on cue, do not attempt fake crying. Loud sobs using your best ugly crying face will probably look more comical than raw and authentic. The same goes for intense anger. Are you able to show rage authentically or are you planning to just scream and shout with your arms flailing around you? If you're not convincing, you run the risk of looking silly.

You can relate to the character

Your performance will be more believable if you have chosen a monologue said by a character you understand and can relate to. Think about the age, gender and ethnicity of this character. Would you be a believable fit for this role? Can you personally relate to their thoughts and experiences? The more closely a monologue speaks to you, the more you'll be able to authentically embody the character and deliver a believable performance. Remember, I'm only talking about monologues you might use for an audition or to impress an agent. That's not to say that one day you might portray a character who is very different from who you are.

It's inoffensive

There are some world-famous monologues out there that use some pretty coarse language, crass jokes or offensive remarks. Samuel L Jackson delivers a couple of phenomenal monologues in *Pulp Fiction*, but they are littered with F-bombs. The monologues in the script of *Spamalot* are considered hilarious by some and crude by others. It's true that someone might be offended no matter what you choose, but you probably ought to stay away from material that is openly offensive.

It has a structure

Choose a monologue that takes the viewer on a journey. You start somewhere and you end somewhere else. It should show a shift in the character's thought process. One of the reasons Ellen Burstyn's monologue in *Requiem for a Dream* (the red dress) is so powerful is that she takes us on an emotional rollercoaster as she talks about her chance to be on a television show.[43] She starts hopeful, descends into despair and climbs back to a fragile sense of hope.

---

43 Movieclips. (2012, May 22). *The Red Dress – Requiem for a Dream (6/12) Movie CLIP (2000) HD* [Video]. YouTube.

The Red Dress Monologue

It's not famous

As I said before, there are many famous monologues you can draw inspiration from, but I would stop short of using them in an audition space or for impressing agents. I touched on this in the chapter on showreels, but it's worth repeating. Your attempt at Sally Field's monologue from *Steel Magnolia* is only going to put you in a position of being directly compared to Sally Field, and that's less than ideal.[44] Even if you do an amazing version of her monologue, the people watching can't avoid running the existing scene in their head. You want them to be appreciating your craft and not thinking about the material.

Sally Field's Monologue

---

44 Child of the 80s. (2018, September 2). *1989 – Steel Magnolias – M'Lynn's Breakdown (Sally Field)* [Video]. YouTube.

Theatre also has its share of overdone monologues you're best to steer clear of. Shakespeare monologues, for example, can be overused, but sometimes casting directors ask actors specifically to do a Shakespeare monologue because they want to see how you master the distinct language used in his plays and that you understand it. Shakespeare monologues are difficult (in my opinion), and they're important to get right.

It's not written by you

I covered in chapter five how writing your own movie scripts can help you as an actor, so I am definitely not trying to discourage your creative endeavours. I'm saying that a monologue you have written yourself may not be the best choice for your audition. I've had actors audition for me with their own monologues, and each resembled a ramble. I'm sure there are many wonderful monologues that actors have written themselves, and I just haven't had the pleasure of hearing them yet. However, I've not yet seen this option work out for an actor, so I encourage you not to use a monologue from your own project.

Performing your monologue

It might seem like one big long speech, but it's not. Each line needs to be carefully considered regarding its delivery. Think about each one and decide how your character will speak. What emotion will you start with? Which line will be the point where your emotional state changes or where a thought enters your mind that changes the direction of your monologue? Where in the monologue will you speed up your delivery or, perhaps, slow it down? What will you do at specific points as you speak? Is there a line that requires a frown? A smile? A nervous laugh or frustrated sigh? Sounds, facial expressions and pauses all add to your delivery, and they are required because a monologue is all you and no one else.

Introduce yourself

Nerves can get the best of us in this business, to the point where an actor might come into an audition and forget to introduce themselves and the piece they are about to perform. Casting directors have a lot of people to get through and will be looking for a reason to say no, so don't give them one by launching straight into your scene without even introducing yourself.

Watch your pace

I know I said earlier not to make the monologue too long, but that doesn't mean you should speak quickly. You don't get extra points for reciting the whole monologue in record time. I've seen this happen time and again, and I've also done it myself. You might not feel like you have the luxury to pause between lines, but seriously, take a breath. You want to be a believable character, and the truth is that people do not move through life talking at warp speed. We pause when we're thinking, we laugh when we're nervous, we groan when we're angry. The only reason you should speak in a rush is if your character is actually panicked or has some reason to get their words out quickly.

Don't forget to move

Just because there's nothing else on stage but you and your words doesn't mean you need to stand still in a spotlight. At the same time, you don't need to fill the space with lots of over-the-top gestures and arm waving unless you think that's what your character would actually do. There are all sorts of ways we communicate our thoughts and moods. From putting our hands to our head to shrugging our shoulders, there are a plethora of ways to speak with our bodies. Test out the different ways you might move your body as you say these words. Find authentic motions for your character and the situation they're in. If the monologue you've chosen has come from an existing film or television show, you do not have to mimic the performance of that actor. You could play around with different deliveries to bring your own take to it. However, ensure you do not lose the context of the story by changing the delivery too much. It still has to make sense.

Are you talking to me?

It's important to be clear about who you're talking to and where they are in the room before you begin. Determining this will help you work out where to look while you act. Let's break down the possibilities:

Talking to someone else

Before you start this scene, take some time to understand who you're speaking to. Who are they? What is their story? What is the relationship between you? Really feel that dynamic so your delivery is appropriate. Once you've decided on the tone and intensity you'll bring, imagine them in the room and decide where they'll be.

Make a plan about how you'll set up your scene. If there are two characters in the room with you when you're saying your monologue, you might put your bag in one spot and put a chair in another. Make it clear that these objects represent the two people in the scene.

Picture the people you're talking to standing or sitting in the spots you've chosen. Imagine their reactions as you talk. Are they listening, are they defensive, or are they showing emotion? In turn, you should say your lines in response to what you see in your mind's eye. Although you are the one doing all the talking, the other person is important in this kind of monologue. They are the reason you're speaking, so you need to act like they are truly there.

Talking to the audience

This is known as 'breaking the fourth wall'. Generally, plays, movies and television shows go to great lengths to make the audience forget they are watching something artificial. Why would a playwright or director choose to break this illusion by having the actor address the audience? Sometimes, it's a storytelling mechanism. In the musical *Fiddler on the Roof*, the main character, Tevye, speaks to the audience directly throughout to give greater context to the story. Sometimes, it's done to foster a closer relationship between the audience and the character. If you want a good movie example of this, put *Ferris Bueller's Day Off* on your viewing list. You can't help but root for Ferris to get away with all his mischief because he shares his feelings so deeply with the audience as he goes along. The comedic shows *Fleabag* and *Miranda* are great television examples.

Even though you are speaking to the audience, you wouldn't say your lines directly to the casting director or an audition panel. They are trying to critique you, and they don't want to deal with the intensity of being spoken to directly. Pick a spot in the room that's just above their eye line so you can talk to the audience without talking to your actual audience.

Talking to yourself

This is called a soliloquy, and though often linked to Shakespearean plays, they appear in more modern works too, such as Robert De Niro's famous 'Are you talking to me?' scene.[45] It might seem like a strange storytelling technique, but writers have their reasons for using them. They help an audience understand the internal voice of a character, and they can help clarify the decisions a character makes or provide otherwise hidden information. It can be harder to make it obvious that you're talking to yourself and not someone else in these kinds of scenes.

Robert DeNiro "Are you talking to me?"

Essentially, a soliloquy is spoken to the audience, but not in the same way as breaking the fourth wall. You see, when you speak to the audience by breaking the fourth wall, you are acknowledging them, and you might even react to them if, for example, they were to laugh at what you say. When you speak to the audience via a soliloquy, you do not see the actual audience but rather an audience full of mirrors. You would not notice or react to anything the real audience does. A soliloquy is not

---

45 Movieclips. (2014, January 15). *Taxi Driver (5/8) Movie CLIP – You Talkin' to Me? (1976) HD* [Video]. YouTube.

always said to the audience. It depends on the script. In the play and movie *Shirley Valentine* (which I personally love), the main character talks to the walls in her house.

Generally, a soliloquy could be a confusing option for an audition, unless you find one where it's really clear that you're talking to yourself (or the walls in the case of *Shirley Valentine*).

Performing memorised monologues will serve you as an actor in many ways. Not only will they help you keep your memorising skills fresh, they will also help you learn how to carry a scene. But memorising and saying them frequently in front of the mirror will not be enough. Make sure you perform them in front of people too, so you can practise bringing a full-bodied expression when the time comes.

To give an even more impressive performance, you might go a step further and memorise a monologue in an accent to show the diversity of your skills. Mastering some accents will definitely assist you in your acting career, and we cover this in the chapter ahead.

CHAPTER THIRTEEN

Learn an Accent

Anyone who knows me knows I adore accents and the fun actors can have with them. I love learning accents so much that I created my own method of teaching them, started my own accent coaching business, and have now become known online as the 'Accent Queen'.

But why do I love accents? What drew me to acting in the first place was that it allows me to be a million different people to a million different people. Accents give me a greater ability to embody a person completely different from myself, and they can give you that chance too.

What is an accent?

Your accent is one part of your dialect, which is also made up of grammar, syntax and vocabulary. An accent refers to the distinct sounds you make as you pronounce words. If we gathered a group of people from around the world and asked them to each say the same sentence in English, there would be variances in their delivery. This is because their accents cause them to make particular sounds differently, such as rounding their vowel sounds or extending their Rs.

In general, an accent is specific to a group of people who live within a particular geographic location. People who move away from that area will generally retain their accent, but their children may adopt a softened version depending on how much time they speak and listen to people with accents different from their family.

How will learning an accent help me?

It might seem like accents are just an added bonus to have on your CV, and of course they are, but they will also help you in other ways you might not have considered.

Mastering an accent stretches you as an actor. Remember how we talked about the fact that having your lines memorised properly will let you just concentrate on the performance? Well, imagine now also having to memorise those lines in an accent. It's another ball to juggle as you deliver your performance, and learning how to do this while remaining in character adds another layer to your skill set. Even though it truly is a skill to deliver an authentic accent in character, it can be under-appreciated by industry leaders who simply expect that actors will know how to do this.

Sometimes casting calls go out with little notice. If the part requires an accent, you'll be well ahead of your competition if you have already mastered it. Too many actors say to me 'I'll learn one if I need to', but you're kidding yourself if you think you can master an accent in the blink of an eye. Booking in for some emergency dedicated one-to-one sessions with an accent coach before the audition might help you sound convincing enough on the day, but will that leave you enough time to be able to move and act while you deliver the accent? If it's a self-tape (which we cover in Act III), you might get away with delivering the accent on video without too much movement, but you'll still be expected to bring emotion, facial expressions and gestures to the scene. These could easily throw your accent off if you haven't had enough time to practise doing all of it at once.

Which accents should you learn?

If you've taken the time to master some accents, you won't be worried about trying to fudge your way through an audition. Instead, you can spend your time memorising the lines and perfecting your delivery. Sounds great, but which accents should you have up your sleeve?

Five Accents Every Actor Needs to Master

I love all accents, but the Standard American English and Standard British English accents are probably the two you should start with as an actor.

Standard American English

If you are American, you're possibly thinking that there is no such thing as a standard American accent. The British say the same thing about the idea of a standard British accent too. Truthfully, probably every country in the world is insulted by the idea that there is one accent an actor could use to portray all the people from their country. In answer to that, I would say it really has a lot to do with the story being told.

Sometimes, where people are from plays an important part of the story, such as the characters in *West Side Story*. Other times, the focus is 100% on the plot, and it could really be set anywhere. Take a teen flick, for example, like *Sixteen Candles*. It's an American coming-of-age cult classic, but ultimately where that story is set isn't important for the viewer (it's set in Chicago, in case you didn't know). For these kinds of stories, American actors often work on trying to reduce or soften their natural accent, so although they sound American, it's not easy to work out where in America they are from. That's what makes it the Standard American accent. If you know your regional accents well and listen carefully, there might be a word or two that, when said, will point you to their home state.

But why should you learn the Standard American accent? Well, because we live in a globalised society. Studios are no longer limited to shoot in their own countries. If it's cheaper to film in another country or the location is important in the story, they will pack up their cameras and jump on a plane. So, no matter where you are in the world, an American movie or TV show could be filming in your neck of the woods. There could well be a casting call for local actors to take part and you want to be ready with your perfected Standard American accent.

Standard British English

Okay, here we go again with being general. The same applies to this accent as it does to the Standard American. If your character is from a certain part of Britain and this is an important part of the plot, then by golly you need to explore that part of Britain and learn the distinct accent of the area. And I don't just mean London. There are multiple accents in that city alone, so if your character is from London, it pays to ask from where in London exactly, so you can be specific. But if the plot only requires you to be noticeably British but not from a distinct area, then this would call for the Standard British accent. The nondescript British accent is turning up in movies and television shows around the world, so it's worth giving it a try.

Why should actors care about accents?

If you, like me, want to be a million different people to a million different people, then you need to be open to playing someone far different from yourself. Being willing to learn accents and using them authentically will broaden your acting options, but you have to use them correctly.

In general, I have found that people do not like hearing someone putting on an accent from their country. This could be because actors sometimes exaggerate the accent slightly to get the sounds right in their mouth. This can result in an over-the-top accent that sounds off to the people from that region. Actors do need to project the accent they use so it's audible to the audience, but it is important not to overdo it, otherwise you will sound cartoonish or stereotypical. Here are some more points to keep in mind:

Bad accents break movies

There aren't many movies out there with bad accents that performed well at the box office. There is one fundamental reason for this. If the accent is unconvincing, the viewer cannot suspend their disbelief and enjoy the movie. That's it. You cannot act your way out of a bad accent. Some movies with terrible accents might actually have been good if they had just left them out altogether, and many movies do. Take the movie *Gladiator*, for example; Russell Crowe was supposed to be playing a Roman general from 180 AD. What sort of accent would have been historically accurate? If historical accuracy had been paramount, they probably would have had the characters speaking Latin and using subtitles. But they did not want an accent to distract from the story, and no one complained except maybe some historians. His natural Australian accent would definitely not have worked, so he opted for a British accent, which most accepted due to the regality of his position in the story. Colin Farrell opted to use his natural Irish accent in the movie *Alexandra*, which was completely out of place for the story he was telling. His co-star Angelina Jolie attempted to sound Greek but ended up sounding Russian, which, again, was quite out of place in the Macedonian desert.[46]

Colin Farrell and Angelina Jolie in *Alexandra*

A bad accent can haunt you

If you were to do an Internet search of the worst accents in movies, you would probably see the same names over and over. Most commonly mentioned is American Dick Van Dyke's

---

46 Warner Bros. Entertainment (2014, May 23). *Alexander: The Ultimate Cut | Theatrical 10th Anniversary – Behave | Warner Bros. Entertainment* [Video]. YouTube.

attempt at a Cockney accent in *Mary Poppins*, which he still apologises about to this day. He has been awarded Tonys, Emmys and been inducted into the Television Hall of Fame, and yet his terrible accent from *Mary Poppins* continues to follow him around. It's important to note that accent coaches were unheard of when that movie was made, so I think we all ought to cut Dick some slack for doing his best. In any case, the movie is still a much-loved production around the world today.

Many famous actors continue to do amazing work despite crashing out with a bad accent. Leonardo DiCaprio, for example, is still a revered actor despite failing at several accents, including the Irish accent in *Gangs of New York* and the Rhodesian accent in *Blood Diamond* (though I actually thought he did okay in that movie despite the backlash). The point is, if you're going to do it, try your very best to land it rather than crossing your fingers that no one will notice.

The people who get the most annoyed at bad accents are those who hail from the location you are trying to portray. The movie *Crouching Tiger, Hidden Dragon* was a huge success in America but bombed terribly in China. The four main characters all spoke Mandarin but used different accents. This was something keenly noticed by the Chinese audience, who were not impressed.[47]

A good accent can be career defining

I've covered the dangers of delivering a bad accent, but on the flip side, nailing a convincing accent can only serve you as an actor. Some actors are so amazing at their accent delivery that

---

47 Schaefer, S. (2022, March 23). *Filming Crouching Tiger, Hidden Dragon Was A Constant Struggle Behind The Scenes*. Slashfilm.

people are genuinely shocked to hear them speak in their natural voice. Toni Collette is a great example. Many people forget she is Australian until she's interviewed by the media. People are also surprised to learn that Christian Bale is British because of the number of American roles he's played.

One of my favourite shows for accents is *Killing Eve*. Jodie Comer is an absolute accent genius. At the premiere of Season Two, she told the press that her love of accents started as a child watching TV: 'If there was an advert with a silly voice on, we'd always impersonate it around the house, just joking around.'[48] Impersonation will only take you so far when learning an accent, but it can be a fun way to start, as Jodie found. To become more authentic, you will need to do further research into the distinct sounds of the accent and then also other aspects of dialect. Another interesting point she shared in her interview was that she found accents allowed her to more fully step into her character and out of her everyday persona. So, in that way, an accent can help you better connect with your role and aid you in your acting delivery. Just like Toni Collette, many people are blown away to hear Jodie speak in her natural Scouse accent from her home town of Liverpool.

How to approach learning an accent

As I mentioned, an accent coach can help you with grasping the key sounds of an accent and delivering them authentically. If you're thinking about going down that path, I know a really good one (wink, nudge, check out my website).

---

48 Miller, A. (2019, May 15). *Jodie Comer reveals how she became the accent queen as Villanelle in Killing Eve, thanks to her father.* Metro.

My Accent Coaching Website

I appreciate, however, that not everyone has the means to pay for those services. So here are a few pointers as you start to explore learning an accent:

Act first, then layer an accent

At an audition, first and foremost you need to show that you can act. When actors forget to embody the fullness of their character and are preoccupied with nailing an accent, industry professionals refer to this as 'acting the accent'. The result is a dry performance with a strong accent, and that's not ideal. Generally, casting are not auditioning for an accent alone, they're looking for a portrayal of the entire character, the whole package. If your accent is spot on but you do a terrible job on the acting, you won't get through; it truly is the acting that comes first. And though I have a passion for accents, I am also passionate about acting, and bad acting with a great accent is not a winning combination. If you do an amazing job and look just like the character they have in mind, they might be willing to pay for an accent coach. It all depends on the budget of the production.

Immerse yourself

This means living and breathing the accent you are trying to master. If you can be around people who speak in this accent naturally, that would help immensely. Though your family and friends might find it a bit funny and awkward, you could try adopting the accent for everyday life, so it becomes your natural way of talking.

Learn the language of the country

If you're as dedicated as Meryl Streep, you might opt to learn the native language of the country. She learned Polish to help her deliver a convincing accent in *Sophie's Choice.*[49] You might consider this a bit of an extreme approach, but you'll recall that in Chapter Ten I explained how learning a language as a special skill can help you as an actor.

Watch the greats

I've already mentioned several actors who hit their accent out of the park. Make watching their work a part of the viewing plan we discussed in Chapter Nine. Play around with mimicking and impersonation. This might work well for your audition, but do run it past someone first. You might think you can do a really good impersonation of late Queen Elizabeth II, but find a brutally honest British person to listen to it first.

---

49 Carlson, E (2019) *Queen Meryl: The Iconic Roles, Heroic Deeds, and Legendary Life of Meryl Streep.* Hachette Books.

Look for free resources from accent coaches

> Plenty of us offer free tips and advice on our websites and social media platforms. Do some research and see if you can get some gold from the Internet. Just check the credentials of whoever you're learning from first (especially for YouTube videos).

Accent stereotypes

In the acting world, there is more talk than ever before about appropriate casting decisions. It's true that in an imaginary world, anyone can be anyone, but we must also consider the social impact casting decisions can make, especially for representation.

We live in a time where more people are feeling empowered to speak up about harmful portrayals in the media. The Netflix documentary *Disclosure*, for example, explores the negative stereotypes commonly used in movies when using a transgender character.[50] At the same time, they spoke positively about what it has meant to see transgender people in movies at all.

Clip from *Disclosure*

---

50 Feder, S (Director). (2020) *Disclosure* [Film] Netflix

It's something to be mindful of when exploring accents. This topic has been specifically explored in the documentary *The Problem with Apu* starring Hari Kondabolu and directed by Michael Melamedoff.[51] Apu is a character of Indian descent depicted in the cartoon comedy *The Simpsons*. The character is voiced by a white American - Hank Azaria. *The Simpsons* programme depicts many, many cultural stereotypes that are problematic, and Apu is one who features quite regularly. According to the documentary, casting directors have specifically asked actors of Indian descent to use Apu's accent as part of their audition. This was also covered in the *Master of None* television series in an episode called 'Indians on TV'.[52] Aziz Ansari (who created the show) plays a struggling actor, Dev Shah. In this episode, he takes a stand against putting on an exaggerated Indian accent at auditions.

Clip from *Master of None*

He also shares his disappointment in learning that although the main character in the 1986 movie *Short Circuit* is Indian, the role was played by a white American, Fisher Stevens, who was wearing black face.

The discourse around this has boiled down to an important question. Just because an actor could play a different ethnicity, should they? Especially

51 Melamedoff, M (Director). (2017) *The Problem with Apu* [Film] truTV
52 Ansari, A, Yang, A, Jarman, Z (Writers). Wareheim, E (Director). (2015, November 6) *Indians on TV* (Episode 4, Season 1 Master of None).

when actors from that ethnic background are under-represented on stage and in film.

By challenging the status quo and through healthy debate, greater discussion has rippled through the industry. So much so that, in 2021, both Hank Azaria and Fisher Stevens genuinely apologised publicly for contributing to stereotyping and marginalising southeast Asian people.[53]

Accents have also been used to make commentary about class, and this has also been called out in recent times. People from the southern states of America, for example, are getting fed up with their accent being used to portray ignorant or uneducated people. It just doesn't fly anymore, and it really is for the best.

You can have as much fun with accents as you like, but for auditioning and casting, I recommend you concentrate your efforts on accents from ethnicities you are likely to be cast in.

The audition

If you don't have a lot of time to get an accent perfected for your audition, I tell my clients to make sure they start and finish strong. If you fudge the beginning, it's likely you will be passed over. Remember, as soon as the accent breaks, the scene breaks, so don't start broken. Get them hooked at the beginning, do your best through the middle and finish strong so you stick in their minds.

If the audition specifically requests an accent to be used as part of the audition, then it's important to the plot. You have to deliver it. Put the work in, practise it and deliver it confidently. You may think it's brave of

---

53 Towers, A. (2021, May 11). *Fisher Stevens regrets doing brownface in Short Circuit: 'It definitely haunts me'*. Entertainment Weekly.

you to wing it, but there are no extra points for taking a shot in the dark. Doing a poor attempt is only going to hurt your future chances if you are deemed a time waster.

Do you have to learn an accent?

I personally think it's a good idea and could bring you more opportunities, but no, you don't have to learn one. There are some actors who have made their natural accent their calling card, such as Sofia Vergara, who has a thick yet natural Colombian accent that she's kept for her role as Gloria on *Modern Families*. Holly Hunter has kept her natural accent in many roles and Arnold Schwarzenegger also opted to keep his natural accent for his work. Actors sometimes try to reduce their natural accents, but for some it's too ingrained, so they work with it instead of against it.

The rise of accent coaches

Studios are starting to take the authenticity of accents more seriously by employing accent coaches. I've been asked to work on sets a handful of times as an accent coach, but ultimately my services are still seen as a 'nice to have'. Sometimes, I was not given nearly enough time to work with the actors. It can be incredibly difficult if the director yells 'Cut! That was amazing!' while I'm thinking *No, the accent was totally off.*

Unfortunately, whether the actor has got the accent right isn't always prioritised, as you can tell from the many famous actors who have delivered terrible accents. It's crazy that no one on set noticed, for example, the lucky charm Irish accent Tom Cruise used in the movie *Far and Away*.[54] Perhaps no one felt they could tell him? The result was that

54 Howard, R (Director). (1992) *Far and Away* [Film] Universal Pictures.

no one could take the movie seriously with what was almost a comical accent.

Clip from Far and Away

How many of these movies with bad accents would have been triumphs if an accent coach had been on set? It's hard to say for sure because the accents weren't always the only thing terrible about these movies. I can only hope the trend of bringing in professionals like me will continue to grow as the importance of authentic accents is more widely recognised.

I mentioned before that one-to-one accent coaching can be out of reach financially for some actors, and it can be difficult to carve out time to get to lessons. That's why I also offer accent courses online, and in fact, many different aspects of acting are now taught via the Internet. Not sure if online learning is for you? Explore it with me in the chapter ahead.

CHAPTER FOURTEEN

Online Learning

I f attending university or going to a performing arts school is not something you can do due to time, money or other constraints, then online learning might be a really good option for you. I personally enjoy learning online, because I'm a visual learner. I'd much rather learn via video than pens and paper.

It doesn't matter if you're in the remotest part of the world, if you have an Internet connection, then you have the world at your fingertips. Whatever it is that you want to learn, there is almost certainly an online course for it, and that includes acting.

The changing landscape of learning

Many might assume that acting classes can only be done in person because of the physical nature of the profession, but actually, there is a lot that can be taught online (though not without some challenges). The COVID-19 pandemic pushed a lot of institutions to create online offerings, and many of them remain on offer, as they allow a greater reach for enrolment.

The benefits of online learning

Online learning opens up possibilities for aspiring actors in many ways. Here are just some of the advantages signing up for an online course can provide:

Accessibility

Depending on where you live, travelling to in-person classes can be a challenge. Maybe you don't have your own transport or parking is dismal. These travel-related barriers can be removed thanks to online training. Access can be as easy as walking from your bedroom to your home office or even pulling out your phone. I'd take that over sitting in traffic or circling the city for a parking space.

Go at your own pace

Not all of us can put our lives on hold and focus on studying for extended periods of time. We may have jobs to hold down or families to take care of. My life is insanely busy, so I need studying to fit around my life. Courses with pre-recorded material that can be watched when time allows work really well for me.

Targeted learning

You can take a comprehensive course on acting in general, or you can find someone who teaches the specific skills and knowledge you're looking for. For example, many of my students have taken acting classes but enrol in my online courses to learn a particular accent. I also run a 'self-tape academy' for actors wanting to improve their self-tape technique (self-tapes are covered in chapter eighteen). Online learning options allow you to pick and choose what you want to learn and build knowledge over time.

Oh, the people you'll meet (virtually)

Online courses give students the opportunity to connect with other actors from all over the globe. You might gain an understanding of how their industry differs from your part of the world, or a fellow student might share experiences from their acting journey that you can learn from. These are people you would never have met without an online learning environment. There's potential for all sorts to come out of these connections. For example, you might have noticed some clever collaborations that happened between musicians and actors around the world during COVID-19 lockdowns. The 'Boss B#tch Fight Challenge' by Zoe Bell is an excellent example of global collaboration.[55] If your online course connects you to other people in this way, take advantage of the chance to build a global network.

Boss B#tch Fight Challenge

---

55 Zoe Bell (2020, May 2). *BOSS BITCH FIGHT CHALLENGE – Zoe Bell* [Video]. YouTube.

Affordability

Generally, you should find online courses to be less expensive than in-person training. Many involve pre-recorded lessons, so the teacher can repurpose their knowledge again and again. There is little ongoing cost for the teacher to provide these teachings, so they can, for the most part, provide them at a lower cost. Pre-recorded courses should still provide quality information and content, since they are based on the teacher's years of knowledge and experience.

If the online course you sign up to includes live classes, one-to-one sessions or individual feedback on assignments, then you can expect to pay more than you would for a pre-recorded course. Any course that requires the teacher to be present and interacting with you is using up more of their time and, therefore, will be more expensive. You can still learn a lot without interacting with the teacher, but having the ability to ask questions is a valuable bonus.

Some courses have a mixture of both. Maybe the course includes a certain number of one-to-one sessions that can be booked over a period of time, or maybe there is one live class a week with the rest being pre-recorded. It could be entirely pre-recorded with individual personalised feedback given on the coursework you submit.

If you don't have any budget to pay for an online course, then you can look on platforms such as YouTube for a whole raft of free tutorial videos. Generally, these videos will not be in depth and will likely give you tips rather than full lessons. Some of these tips might be real gold nuggets, so definitely don't dismiss the free information you can find. However, check out the credentials of the person in the video. Anyone can create a tutorial and upload it online, whether they actually know what they're talking about or not.

Give something new a try

For shy students, online training options provide a safe environment to try something new. It can be daunting to try a technique or skill you've never tried before, and perhaps it might be even more intimidating to do this in front of an in-person classroom. I have certainly found this to be true with the students who take my online accent courses. They like working through the material individually and receiving my feedback without other students looking on. Few people land an accent straight off the bat, and no one wants to be embarrassed for trying. My accent courses allow students to dip their toes into an area of acting that many of them might have been too apprehensive to even consider otherwise

Keep learning between gigs

You always want to be working on your craft between gigs. You might not want to lock yourself into intensive studies that will make it hard for you to get to auditions. Online courses can offer a lot of flexibility in terms of when and how you get them done. This lets you keep auditioning and learn more skills as you go.

The camera is already rolling

You've already got your webcam set up for online learning, so now you can use it for acting. There's no point in worrying about being camera shy if you're already on film in front of the class and teacher. It's true webcams aren't great for wide angles and big movements, but they work fine for those up-close-and-personal scenes that require emotional facial expressions. This is the sort of camera work prevalent in TV shows and films.

Train with global superstars

Online learning not only allows you easier access to training provided in your own city or country, it opens you up to attend courses provided by teachers placed all over the world.

Perhaps your goal was to save up enough money to move to New York or London and train with the best in the industry? You could still do that, or…you could sign up for an online course taught by the very people you long to connect with but without upheaving your whole life. There are many industry experts monetising their knowledge by creating quality online courses for a worldwide market.

For example, if you'd like to learn something from actors who have made it big, Morgan Freeman and Natalie Portman both have online masterclass courses. You can also find great courses on offer from other industry experts, like Greg Apps, who is a well-known Australian casting director.

The challenges of online learning

You may love rolling out of bed and studying in your pyjamas, but online learning is not without its disadvantages. You can learn a lot about acting online, but eventually, you will need to put that learning into action on stage or in front of a camera. Those environments are in-person environments and quite different from interacting online.

You need to focus

For many of us, our home is our sanctuary. Being able to learn from the comfort of our sanctuary can feel like heaven on earth. However, it is the comforts of home that can sometimes distract us from what we are supposed to be focusing on. Your home is not a dedicated learning environment, like a classroom. You will need to ignore the call of your laundry basket or your dog sitting with a lead in its mouth. These things would not be in your vista inside a classroom.

Focusing in an online classroom may be easier if it's a live experience and you're required to participate. But again, perhaps the temptation is there to turn off your camera while others are talking to make yourself a cup of tea. Sure, you could zone out in a classroom setting, but you are unlikely to get up and walk out of the room. It's important to be present with your classmates. The feedback you give each other is vital, and you're not going to be able to do that if you aren't paying attention.

Less social interaction

Online courses can definitely be created in a way that encourages and fosters interaction between the students and their teacher, but there's not much to be done about the lack of opportunity for social interaction.

Social interaction is the spontaneous conversations and invitations that happen during lunch breaks or after class. You may really like chatting with the student in your online class from France or Japan, but you cannot meet up for a coffee or go check out a play together. Building social connections is a natural benefit of attending in-person classes, but hey, not everyone makes those kinds of connections in an in-person class, and you never know, you might meet up with that student in France when you finally get the chance to go.

Technology is great - when it works

High-speed Internet and top-notch webcams are great, but sometimes our technology fails us. When you're trying to embody a character and act out a scene, it can be incredibly frustrating when your scene partner has a frozen screen or has lost sound. Hopefully, this won't be a common occurrence, but it is one of those things that comes with operating in an online environment.

You could feel disconnected

The COVID-19 pandemic taught us there is a lot more that can be taught online than previously thought, but some things can only be experienced in person. Acting with another person in the flesh is its own experience. There is a physical, visceral component of being in the same space as another person. Emotion and energy are experienced on a different level. That's not to say that you can't have powerful exchanges with another person via a camera. After all, audiences have their own emotional experiences from watching television shows and films.

Trying to act online via your webcam will restrict the kind of scenes you could play with. Scenes that call for you to move and take up space will need to be reserved for a time that you can be out of your living room (unless, of course, you have a lot of space in your house).

What to look for in an online course

We've covered some great reasons to consider online learning, but it's important to know what you're looking for before signing up. As I said before, anyone (and I mean anyone) can create an online course and start marketing it for sale, so it's on you to look closely at them to be sure you're getting value for money. Here are a few specifics to check:

Who is teaching this course?

Make sure the person you're listening to knows what they're talking about. They should list their credentials and industry experience. Get on the net and research whether they have indeed got the experience they say they have.

Do you want personal interaction?

There are a lot of courses out there providing a wide range of interaction from none to completely interactive. Hopefully, how much personal interaction you'll get as part of the course is outlined in its structure, but if not, just ask. Are you looking for something that is taught live? Do you like the idea of breakout groups that provide interaction between students? Do you want direct feedback from the teacher?

You might find that all the interaction is done via chat boxes or forums. Some people are timid in group situations and actually prefer all interactions to be done via discussion boards if direct communication feels too intense. This can be especially true for people new to a subject or industry. An active discussion board between students around the world can be a fascinating place where questions and ideas are bounced around with lots of potential for collaboration.

Is it mostly self-directed learning?

Being able to learn at your own pace is one thing, but to what level are you left to your own devices to get this course completed? I'm sure many of us can confess to signing up for an online course we didn't finish or perhaps didn't even start. If the course you've signed up to is completely self-directed, are you motivated enough to get it done? Don't fool yourself into thinking that the fact you've paid for the course will be motivation enough. Plenty of us sign up for a year contract at the gym and then hardly ever go, despite money going out of our account every week or month.

If the course you've chosen is completely self-directed, but it's one you really want to do, then I suggest getting organised. Work out your weekly schedule, and plan what days and times you'll allocate for working through the material and/or completing assignments and practical work.

Otherwise, you might prefer to look for courses that have built-in prompts and motivators to keep you going. Some courses only unlock each lesson as you complete the previous one, including uploading or submitting examples of your work. Some will send you a text or email if they notice periods of inactivity on your course. You might be able to connect with other students who are also completing the course. If so, encourage each other, and do what you can to keep each other motivated. Ask each other for help when you get stuck.

What support is available?

Hopefully, the course provides an online support system if you have questions about the material or any technical problems. It's worth checking that there's someone you can contact if you get lost or completely confused.

What will be the end result?

You might do an online course for fun or out of curiosity, and there's nothing wrong with that, of course. If you are doing something a little more serious, then it would be good to know if the course includes any assessments or an end grade. Is there an accreditation you get for completing or points that can go towards a greater qualification? If that's not important to you, then that's fine, but if it is, it's worth checking it's included.

If you're disciplined and self-motivated, online learning might be just the thing for you. You will need to be committed to get the most out of your time and money investment. However, if you need structure, enjoy hands-on learning and want to meet people, you would probably benefit more from an in-person learning environment.

CHAPTER FIFTEEN

Going to Acting School

Not everyone is cut out for learning in a classroom. That was certainly the case for me. I have never been a 'sit in a chair and listen' kind of person. I get that some people are, but for me, it was always a bit of a struggle. I also didn't do great when it came to tests and exams, and the poor results I received diminished my confidence. Thank goodness, times have changed since I was at school, and more is understood about the different ways people learn.

I left school when I was sixteen and moved to London when I was nineteen. I had to support myself financially, which didn't leave me much time for auditions, let alone study. Later on, I enrolled at Bournemouth and Poole College of Art and Design when I was about twenty-two. I studied film production in the hope that, as a producer, I could create my own projects and star in them. I also made the correct assumption that, by going to film school, I'd be surrounded by filmmakers in need of actors for their projects.

Despite my early struggles at school, I eventually found fantastic teachers who brought out the best in me as a performer. I discovered that I have a real thirst for knowledge and became a life-long learner. It turns out that, in the right environment, I'm able to pick up new skills and knowledge really quickly.

Should every actor study acting?

It's true that some of the most amazing actors to grace the big screen went to the best performing arts schools in the world. Actors including:

Cate Blanchett - National Institute of Dramatic Art (NIDA – Australia)[56]

Denzel Washington - American Conservatory Theatre (ACT)[57]

Jim Broadbent - London Academy of Music and Dramatic Arts (LAMDA - London)[58]

Viola Davis - The Juilliard School (New York)[59]

That you want to follow in their footsteps makes perfect sense, and there are many fantastic training institutions in every country around the globe.

Acting Schools Around the World

---

56 All Alumni. Alumni & Industry. NIDA.
57 Prominent A.C.T. Alumni, A.C.T. Alumni, A.C.T.
58 Meet our LAMDA Acting Alumni, Acting Alumni, LAMDA
59 Alums Take home Emmys (October 2015). The Julliard Journal

But remember, there's no single right way to become an actor. Plenty of actors train at institutions, and many do not. In fact, you might be surprised to learn just how many well-known actors never went to acting school, such as Henry Cavill, Meg Ryan and Johnny Depp.[60]

While a prestigious school on your CV will definitely impress industry leaders, it's no walk in the park to complete a qualification at these institutions, and you have to be accepted into their programmes before you even begin. Completing a degree or diploma at a performing arts school or university is a matter of personal preference, finances and acceptance criteria for the programme.

What to look for at an acting school

If you have your heart set on completing some study, take a deep dive on each place you're interested in. Collect their brochures, browse their website, go to their information nights, and get an understanding of their coursework and delivery style. Here are some specific features you might want to check out:

What does their course cover?

Are they things you want to learn? Most acting/drama schools are focused on theatre training, which can be very beneficial for an actor, but may not be your thing. As covered in chapter eight, theatre experience provides actors with a lot of tools and knowledge to round out their skills. But if you know in your heart that you have no interest in stage acting, spending a lot of time and money learning the ways of theatre may not be the best use of your resources.

---

60 Famous Actors who didn't go to Acting School. IMDb.

Some drama/acting schools only provide an overview of the different specific acting techniques. So, if you are interested in learning a particular acting technique, such as Meisner or Stanislavski (which I cover in chapter twenty-seven), you may need to find somewhere that offers dedicated training on that particular technique.

Who's in their network?

You want to have a good grasp on who teaches at this institution (such as their training, credentials and experience). Does the programme include any special guest lecturers from the industry? You may also want to see what you can find out about their past students. Have any well-known actors graduated from their programme? What testimonials/feedback/reviews can you find from past students?

Technology and equipment

When I was at film school, we only had access to big clunky VHS video cameras, and they certainly weren't something we could take home and play with. We could only use them within the classroom, and there were only a few to share within groups. Fortunately, technology has come a long way. It's a good idea to check out if your course teaches you how to use the latest filmmaking equipment and what access students have to studio time and editing software. However, don't get too hung up on the latest equipment. One of the best pieces of technology an actor can have is the phone sitting in your pocket. It allows you to make a movie anytime and anywhere.

Their showcase

The graduating showcases are a big deal for top acting schools. This is when agents swoop in to sign up all the up-and-coming actors to their agencies. The industry showcase is one of the big benefits of training at a respected acting school, but you do need to put on a fantastic showcase when you get there. So, learn well and ensure you wow them when you get the chance. You will also need to have done all the important tasks I've outlined previously, such as headshots (covered in chapter one) and a showreel (covered in chapter four).

What's the cost?

For the most part, formal actor training is not cheap, and if you want to go to the best institute for your profession, then the price is going to be all the higher. If finances are tight, see if scholarships are on offer. Look at student loan offerings from various banks. Do you have to move cities (or countries) to attend? What student accommodation is available? Are there any student support services? Check if your course offers part-time study options, so you can work while studying if you need to.

The worst-case scenario - you don't get in

If you are trying to enrol in the top schools, like the Royal Academy of Dramatic Art (RADA) in London or the Juilliard School in New York, then you need to know that places are limited. To narrow down the thousands of applications they receive, the top schools hold auditions. You don't want this to be the first audition you ever do, so make sure you've been auditioning for as many projects as possible before you get to this point. It might take a few years of reapplying before you get there, so don't put things off. You need to plan for the long haul in terms of getting accepted. Some acting schools offer workshops on audition techniques, which could be a great idea to increase your chances.

If you get that 'we regret to inform you' letter, take a deep breath and remember that some big stars were also rejected by their pick of drama schools, including:

Daniel Craig - rejected by RADA and LAMDA, but was eventually accepted into Guildhall

Hugh Jackman - rejected by NIDA, and later accepted by WAAPA[61]

And, although not an actor, Steven Spielberg was rejected by the University of Southern California's film school…three times. He ended up attending California State University's film school[62]

If you don't nail your application audition, don't give up. They might not have recognised your talent, but it's possible another fantastic training institution will. In the meantime, here are a few things you could do if you're facing the worst-case scenario:

Take a foundational course

There might be a bridging or foundational course you could take that will help you get into the qualification you're aiming for. This will increase the total cost of your study and the time.

---

61 Roach, V. (2015, May 5). *Stars that were rejected by drama school.* News.com. au.

62 Vilhauer, J. (2019, December 31). *Why Speilberg, a Film School Reject, Was Successful Anyway.* Psychology Today.

Have a back-up plan

Look at other training institutions that are not your first choice. They might not be as prestigious, and maybe your favourite actor didn't attend there, but they could still offer a really good programme.

A summer school programme or short course

If you're dead set on this particular training institute, then you might want to see if they offer any short courses that could fulfil your learning goals. Some do intensive courses or summer school programmes. See if you have an easier time getting into these options.

Break down your learning goals

Maybe you don't need a three-year programme? If you just want to fill the gaps in your knowledge base, you could take specific classes that are ideally run by recognised industry leaders. For example, maybe you want help with your auditioning approach? To learn improv skills or a special skill? Find people teaching what you want to know and try that avenue.

The best-case scenario – you get in

Let's pretend for a minute that you are accepted into the top acting school in your part of the world - congratulations! Now the real work starts in terms of getting the most out of your education investment. Here are a few reminders for the journey:

Have fun, but not too much

If you've worked hard to save money for tuition or have had to get a student loan to go after your dream, then make sure you come through for yourself when you begin your studies. Tertiary education offers lots of opportunities to make friends and have fun. It's important to make those connections and enjoy yourself, but don't let that be the only thing you remember when you leave drama school.

Connect

If you're at a top school, then it's likely the people in your classroom are going to go on to be important people in the industry - from directors to casting directors and lead actors. They are your competition, but also your network - don't forget that.

Prepare to work hard

Studying actors are generally immersed in their craft all day, every day, for around three years. You're going to learn to show up day in, day out, and do long days. You'll be doing a lot of projects, so you'll learn to be proactive and how to manage your time and workload. Formal training will help you create a fantastic work ethic and an understanding of professional standards.

The sheer amount of work you'll do in three years will speed up the amount of experience you'll tuck under your belt. You'll be expected to focus on nothing but the productions and projects the course demands. It can be intensive, with little time for audition opportunities, and some institutions may even suggest you get rid of your agent (if you have one) while you focus on studying. It's a big time commitment in terms of being out of the industry. It will be intense, and it may be taxing mentally and emotionally.

Graduating from an acting school will hopefully instil some confidence in your abilities (and we can all do with a confidence boost!). The end of your formal learning is the beginning of your next journey into the industry at large. Take all that newfound confidence and put yourself out there with determination, but remain open to learning even more from the people you work with.

ACT THREE

CHAPTER SIXTEEN

Finding an Agent

Getting an agent is a classic 'chicken and egg' scenario. Agents are looking for actors with experience, and it's difficult to get experience without an agent. That's why I've spent the last two Acts of this book covering things you can do to build your experience, knowledge, connections and training. By the time you're ready to approach an agent, you should have already done a lot of work to build a solid showreel and have enough experience to flesh out your CV.

An actor getting an agent is a bit like a musician being signed to a record label. They can't just walk into Virgin Records and say 'sign me up', they need to capture the attention of the record company first through a combination of hard work, perseverance and networking. The same is true for actors; you have to prove to an agent that you have acting chops, because an agent is paid via commission and that commission depends on you landing roles. They need to feel confident in your skills and abilities before signing you onto their books.

To gain the attention of an agent takes a dedicated effort. Once I had my sights set on a particular job, so I sent a letter to the employer once a week for three months until they finally said 'FINE! We'll see you on Monday.' I was committed and persevered, and you will have to be just as determined. Don't send a quick and dirty email and expect a phone call the next day. This profession requires you to be a go-getter, not a go-sitter.

Do you need an agent?

You can work without one, and many actors do.

That they help you get auditions and negotiate your contracts makes it worth it to get one in my experience. A newbie actor might be offered $500 for a commercial, and they'll jump at the chance to pay their rent that week, all the while being unaware that they could get paid $5,000 for the same kind of work via an agent.

But, ultimately, it is a personal decision that you'll have to make for yourself. Remember, you'll have no choice but to work without an agent at the beginning of your career while you build your experience, whether it's your intention to have one or not.

What does an agent do?

An acting agent works as the middle person between you (the actor) and your employer (a production company). An agent's job is varied, but their main tasks can be broken down as follows:

Growing and maintaining a network

A good agent is well connected. Even if their agency is new to the field and their books are relatively thin, they should have a solid background in the industry. They invest a lot of time and energy into building and maintaining relationships with top-level executives and decision makers.

Submitting actors to casting directors

Agents receive a steady stream of briefs from casting directors on a daily basis. It's their job to sift through them and submit the actors they think are most appropriate for the role. They'll also check that these auditions are legitimate opportunities from reputable studios.

Provide career guidance

Over time, as you get more work, you may develop a close relationship with your agent. To begin with, however, they will be busy trying to get you work, so they'll have less time to chat. If you don't get a role, your agent is not going to be your grief counsellor, but they might give you some advice on skills or techniques you could brush up on. This will be high-level advice; they should not be referring you to specific courses or particular teachers.

Negotiating contracts

Agents take care of the paperwork so you can focus on acting. Plenty of actors negotiate deals without an agent, and this is an option for you. However, it can be incredibly awkward to set the terms of your own employment, especially when it comes to agreeing on how much you will be paid. I've helped actors renegotiate their contracts on more than one occasion because they got steamrolled into accepting less than acceptable terms. Your agent will ensure you are paid fairly as per industry standards.

Agents do their best to negotiate the best terms and conditions possible for your employment. I cover contracts more deeply in chapter twenty-one, but in general, a contract will cover details like transport requirements, accommodation, overtime and more. Read your contract and discuss it with your agent so you fully understand what you are agreeing to. Agents understand legal documents, but they should not give legal advice. I saw a lot of contracts via my talent agency, and if there was ever a clause or wording I wasn't sure about, I'd check it with a lawyer. Agents want to ensure their actors get the best deal. Your agent might provide you with contact details for a lawyer or they may have a lawyer who works in-house. Some unions, like Equity, provide free access to a lawyer, which is very handy (we cover unions later in chapter twenty-two).

Ensuring their actors get paid

Payment for your work goes to your agent, who removes their commission and then submits the rest to you. Chasing payment for work is not a fun task; be glad your agent will take care of this for you.

Researching agents/agencies

Which agent or agency would you like to be signed with? The world is at your fingertips, so get online and do some research to determine who will be the best fit for you. Here are some things you could check specifically:

Are they new to the industry?

Each country has their top agencies with the best and longest reputations, but that doesn't mean you can't sign with someone newer to the field. If you want to be signed by an up-and-coming agency, check their background:

1. Who are the agents at this agency?
2. What is their work background?
3. Check their Facebook page and other social media.
4. Look them up on the Internet Movie Database website (www. imdb.com) to see if they have any credits.
5. Are they mentioned in any film books? E.g., *The Data Book* in New Zealand, *LA411* for California, *The Knowledge Book* in the UK and *The Production Book* in Australia.

Just because someone is relatively new in their role as an agent doesn't mean they haven't got a breadth of experience, knowledge and contacts from working their way up the ranks in the industry. If they're still trying to establish themselves, they will most likely work doubly hard to secure work for their actors to become better known. Either way, the person who ends up being your agent needs to be someone you connect with. You need to feel like you can trust them to look after your career and they'll have your back.

Are they charging you anything?

Beware of any agents who promise you the moon and the stars for a small monthly fee. They should not charge you any sort of joining fee or monthly subscription. Ultimately, it should be free to be on their books because they are paid a commission on the work they help you secure. They might charge for an extra service. For example, when I ran an agency, we charged an optional yearly fee for our actors to have a profile on our website, which included a photoshoot.

Are they part of a guild or association?

Actor agent associations or guilds exist in most countries. For example, in New Zealand, there is the Actors Agents Association of New Zealand. One of its primary objectives is to 'promote and maintain professional standards among actors' agents in New Zealand'.[63] It's reassuring to know that the agency you're trying to sign with has committed to objectives like this.

Agent Guilds and Associations

That isn't to say, of course, that agencies that have not joined local associations or guilds are not legit in their practices. You might just need to do a little more digging to get a feel for the way they work. Check out their website; you might find they have a mission statement, values or a vision published online. Ask around in your acting community if anyone has had any experience with them and if they would recommend signing.

Who's on their books?

There's a lot to be gained by signing with one of the big-name agencies with many celebrities on their books. I signed with one of the top agencies in London for a while, and it was certainly

---

63 Resources. AAANZ.

a thrill for me to know I was with the same agency as actors Maggie Smith and Daniel Craig. It also gave me greater clout and credibility when it came to auditions. So, if you have your heart set on being signed with the best of the best, then go for it. However, I would also caution you not to narrow your sights too much. Consider a range of agencies and keep your options open. When you're starting out, you will be turned down a lot, so be prepared to take what you can get in terms of representation.

What's their commission?

The commission percentage your agent will take from your earnings differs depending on what country you live in. I have seen a range of 10%-20%. This percentage will change as the years pass by, so do some research on what the current average is and check that against what your agent is proposing.

Approaching an agent

Once you've done the groundwork and have chosen an agent or agency you want to sign with, it's time to go get 'em, but how? You can do a lot to improve yourself as an actor while you work towards being discovered. Essentially, you need to keep perfecting your craft while also reaching out to agents and agencies you want to work with. Here are a few things you can try to get their attention:

Send a package

Emailing has become the standard means of communication in today's world, but you don't want your showreel to drown in a sea of emails in an inbox. Be prepared to step outside the box and send a letter in the mail. Even better, pop a bag of lollies/sweets in with your CV/headshots, etc., and send them a package. Parcels have become so rare, and people love getting them. You could even include a printed QR code that will take them to a webpage with your CV and showreel. You can generate custom QR codes or links to help you keep track of which link you sent to which agent. You'll be able to see for yourself if they're going to your website or just eating the lollies and throwing your letter in the bin. Don't expect results overnight. Send different candy with different letters/links regularly so you can see if you're getting their attention. Make the postal service your click funnel and adjust your tactics as you go.

Get out there and meet people

Networking plays a crucial part in the acting industry. Everyone knows the saying 'it's not what you know but who you know'. Essentially, you need to meet the 'who' first so you can show them what you know. In the acting world, there's always something going on where people are meeting up. I'm not just talking about parties. There are improv groups, classes and social meetups that could serve just as well as a place to make important connections. Keep a list of names and phone numbers for every filmmaker, screenwriter, director and actor you meet. You never know who they might be connected to or what project they might do in the future. One day, a contact you've made might refer you to an agent, and the right referral can make all the difference.

Join a play

We covered the benefits of doing amateur theatre in chapter

eight, so feel free to go back and refresh yourself. Your local amateur dramatic society should invite local agents to come and watch any productions they put on.

After you've been signed

Once an agent has signed you to their books, both of you will work hard to secure you work. Listen to any suggestions they may have about updating your headshots, CV, showreel and any extra training they think would help round you out as an actor. You should absolutely start getting regular auditions within your first month, but that does not mean you should kick back and relax. You need to continue improving as an actor, because your agent can only book you the audition; it's your job to land the role. As an agent, it was extremely frustrating to receive calls from my actors complaining about their lack of work when they would not take any of my advice regarding how they could improve their skills. In summary, if you don't get the role, it will not be because of your agent. It's your agent's job to find opportunities for you and to negotiate your contract after you have done the work to secure the role.

Getting an agent might seem like a daunting task, but they do take chances on new actors, especially when they can see that you've done the groundwork and have a committed work ethic. So, keep working hard and respond quickly to your agent, because auditions can come through at the last minute. Working a flexible job and living close to film studio locations can help you in that regard. Let's talk about why in the chapter ahead.

CHAPTER SEVENTEEN

Living and Working While Acting

I f you've been watching movies as per the suggestion in chapter nine, you might have seen a repeating theme of the waitress who quits her job to pursue her singing or acting career in the big smoke (*Burlesque*, *Coyote Ugly* and *A Star is Born*, for example). Despite how wonderfully this goes for the characters in these films, I recommend you take the time to carefully plan your living and work situation before making any big life changes. In my mid-twenties, I inadvertently ended up in a large city with no money and no plan, and it was not the adventure they made it out to be on the big screen at all.

Where to live

The film industry is usually most prominent in the largest city of a country, but there are smaller cities popping up all over the globe that are considered up-and-coming film locations, for example:

Atlanta - USA[64]

---

64 Dockterman, E. (2018, July 26). *How Georgia Became the Hollywood of the South: TIME Goes Behind the Scenes*. TIME.

Manchester - UK[65]
Vancouver - Canada[66]

Look into filming hotspots in your own country, and you might find you don't need to move to your capital city after all.

The popular TV series *The Walking Dead* was filmed in Atlanta, and quite a few of the cast and crew already lived in the state of Georgia.[67] So, you don't necessarily have to move, but it helps to be where the action is or live travelling distance away, at least.

I had the chance to audition for the part of a Scottish woman in the TV series *Outlander*, which usually would have been perfect for me, but I was in Greece at the time. I had to film a self-tape in sweltering heat with a sun-kissed tan. It was clear that I was not a pale, cold Scottish lassie, and I did not get the part. However, that was merely a case of bad timing. If I had been in Devon (which is about three hours south of London), I would have been on the next train to get to that audition.

Travelling to auditions is one thing, but what if you're cast? Those travel costs could really pile up, and production will not meet them unless you land a lead role or it's negotiated as part of your contract. I was able to do that for one of my agency clients. I presented an audition opportunity to him as a body double for a role that required horse-riding skills. I told him he would have to pay for his own flight to attend the audition, but his chances were high if he went. He took the opportunity, paid his way

---

65 Lodderhose, D. (2022, June 23). *Hot Spots: How Manchester Is Fast Becoming A Magnet For International Productions* DEADLINE.
66 *Why the World's Biggest Movies and TV Shows are Filmed and Produced in B.C.* BCBUSINESS.
67 Summerlin, D. (2014). The Walking Dead. In *New Georgia Encyclopedia.* Retrieved June 8, 2017.

there, and when he got the part, the production company paid for his accommodation costs after that. That was a situation where the cost of travelling to an audition paid off, and that's the kind of choice you may need to make too if you live out of town.

Moving away from your home to a big, noisy, bustling and possibly dirty city could be a big culture shock. You need to be sure about the move before you do it. Reality can be a stark comparison to a glittering dream, so make sure you have a good understanding of what to expect, and be prepared to be uncomfortable for the first few months.

Make a five-year plan

Planning is rarely a strength for creative people. Perhaps that's the reason for all the movies about singers and actors who spontaneously yet recklessly move to a city with only a few dollars in their pockets. It may seem like a drag, but actually working out what you want to achieve and planning how to get there will keep you motivated. It's great to have big lofty goals, but they can be overwhelming when you have no idea how you will achieve them. So, write those big dreams down, maybe at the top of a piece of paper, and write your current situation at the bottom. Now it's time to work out all the steps you'll need to take to climb your way from the bottom of the page to the top.

Moving to London or New York is actually not the first step you need to take (though it might seem like it is). First, you need to work out how you will pay your way to get there and where you're going to live when you arrive. You might not be able to get a job until you get there, and it might take you a while to find one, so how are you going to support yourself while you're looking? Nobody is saying you shouldn't go after your dreams; you just need to be responsible and smart about the decisions you make so that your main concern will be landing auditions and not how (or if) you're going to eat.

Before you move

Broadway may be calling your name, but if you're living comfortably right now and your job lets you put some savings away, then you are best to stay put until you have enough money saved up to make the move easily. But how much money are you going to need? It will take some research to work that out, and here are the questions you should start with:

Do you know anyone there?

Any family or friends, perhaps? It would help you a lot to crash somewhere while you search for a place to live and for a job. If you get along well with these people, maybe you could pay rent and board with them? Have a frank conversation upfront. You don't want to ruin any relationships by overstaying your welcome, and you may find you really do need a place of your own.

If you don't know a soul in the location you want to move to, then consider reaching out online. Look for groups or communities in the acting sphere that can give you some tips and advice. What part of town do they recommend you live in? What are their average living costs?

If the city you want to move to isn't too far away, maybe you could go and spend a day or two checking it out? Where are the acting schools, theatres and film studios located? Get your bearings.

How are you going to get around?

Another thing to research or check out on a visit is the public transport system. You want to be able to navigate your way around this city easily so you can get where you need to be on time. If you have a car, that's great, but what's the parking like in this city? Is it more costly to have a car than to use public transport? In some cities, everyone walks everywhere; in other cities, places are so spread out that having a car is vital.

What's the visa situation?

Moving from a small town to a big city in your own country is a big step to take, but moving to another country is a gigantic one. You will need to make a lot of preparations before you book your flight, starting with determining what kind of work permit or visa you need. Every country is different, so check online what the requirements are and if you're even eligible. If you have contacts in the country you want to move to, they may be able to help as sponsors for your visa.

If you are fortunate enough to be cast in an overseas production after submitting an amazing self-tape, the production company will usually arrange a visa for you, such as the 'artist visa' used by Hollywood studios for overseas actors.

Flexible work

Actors generally find it easiest to take shift work (common in hospitality and retail) because of its flexibility. These jobs are often referred to in the biz as 'survival jobs' because they help you survive while you audition and you can go back to them between gigs.

Working shifts usually means that when an audition comes up, you can hopefully swap with someone else on the roster. If you've already been working in a job like this, it will probably be easiest to find similar work in your new location because you'll have relevant work experience and hopefully glowing references. If you haven't done shift work before and you've been finding it hard to get to auditions, moving to a new city could be a chance for you to start working in these kinds of roles. Unfortunately, a lot of these service jobs are low paid, and if the city you're moving to is flooded with actors, you may find the job market competitive. Doing that research on rent, groceries and other bills for where you want to live will tell you approximately how tight your budget will need to be. Not all job listings include a pay rate, but hopefully enough will so you can work out an average. In some countries, like America, service workers rely heavily on tips to supplement their wages, so take that into consideration.

If you think being a waiter or a cashier would drain the life force out of you, you don't have to force yourself to work in a job you hate. If you have saved up enough money to support yourself for a while, you could take a little more time to find an entry-level job in the TV, movie or theatre industries. Jobs like working front of house as an usher or as a runner on a film set. Alternatively, you could find jobs that utilise your acting skills, such as being a tour guide or children's party entertainer (don't laugh, Hugh Jackman started out as a kids' party clown).[68]

---

68 The Howard Stern Show. (2018, November 13). *Hugh Jackman Recalls His Days Working as a Clown* [Video]. YouTube.

Hugh Jackman Interview

Hugh Jackman is certainly not alone in his experience; I too worked as a clown when I left high school and started my studies at the South Devon College of Art and Design. I was 'Polly Wolly the Silly Dolly' at a local water slide park and to this day I do not understand why we insist on dressing as clowns for kids. So many children are terrified of clowns; I think I did more traumatising than entertaining.

There are even companies that employ actors to take part in role play training at corporations. You'll need to be proactive and take a good look at your options.

It's really important that your survival job sustains you and doesn't suck your will to live. If you are desperate to land a role so you can quit your horrible day job, then you will bring that energy to your audition and everyone can feel it. There are probably more options out there than you think, from being an Uber driver to freelance writing or virtual admin and temp work.

If you already have work experience and knowledge in a particular industry that's not related to acting, you could ask if you could do your job remotely. Not all jobs can be done remotely, but a lot more can since the arrival of COVID-19. Or if the only jobs you can find in your area of expertise require you to work specific hours at a specific location, then you could ask your employer if they would let you take time off as required to attend auditions. You never know, they might be supportive.

No one said it would be easy

I know what it's like to have a dream that just won't leave you alone. It's a dream that drives us to move to unfamiliar cities and work whatever jobs that allow us to get to auditions. Trying to pay the bills while also trying to make it as an actor is no small task. Sometimes, it can come down to going to an audition or keeping your job, and that's an incredibly tough position to be in. I'm sure there are few who envy us, and I was certainly envious myself of people who had support or financial freedom.

If you're fortunate enough to have someone in your life who can support you financially while you pursue acting, that would be ideal. Few of us live in ideal situations, though. Mostly, working out how to survive in a big city as a hopeful actor will require you to plan, save, budget and walk a tightrope between work and auditioning. Hopefully, you'll find a support network of sympathetic fellow actors who share your plight and keep you motivated in your quest.

Until then, let me comfort you with a list of famous actors and the odd jobs they did while they worked towards landing their big break:

Sandra Bullock – bar tending
Chris Rock – bus boy at Red Lobster
Rachel McAdams – McDonalds worker
Denzel Washington – swept hair at a barber shop
Julia Roberts - scooped ice-cream[69]

As for me, I used to wash car windscreens by day and sell roses at local

---

69 Finn, N. (2023, June 25). *These Stars' First Jobs Are So Relatable (Well, Almost)*. *ENEWS*.

bars by night. We all start somewhere. If you don't hate it and it gives you the freedom and support to pursue acting, that's all that matters.

If you can't move or have to work full time because you have family obligations or any other reason, then so be it. Don't let anyone tell you that you're not passionate enough. Only privileged people who have lost touch with just how ridiculously hard it is to make it in this industry say that sort of thing. Maybe you can only do self-tape auditions while you work towards moving house or finding a more flexible job, and that's fine. You can put all your remaining energy into nailing a great self-tape audition, and we'll cover how next.

CHAPTER EIGHTEEN

Self-Tape Auditions

I remember the first time I was asked to do a self-tape audition; it caught me completely off guard. I was running around at the last minute getting a camera and working out how to edit the footage. It was stressful. If you need to do a self-tape audition, you won't magically know how to do it if you've never done it before. You'll be lucky if you've got a week to get it submitted. It could even be needed the next day. If you've been practising self-taping and you're quick at picking up scripts (see chapter eleven, 'Strengthen Your Memory'), you won't be stressed by a tight deadline. Practising even when you don't have an audition coming up might seem like a lot of work, but perfecting your self-tape skills will set you up for success.

About self-tape auditions

A self-tape audition is when an actor films themselves doing a scene (or scenes) and submits it to casting instead of going to a location and auditioning in person. Self-tape auditions allow casting directors to widen their search and include people across an entire country or even around the world.

When the COVID-19 pandemic hit the globe, self-taping became THE way to audition. Everybody had to do it. Around that time, I set up a self-tape academy to teach actors around the world how to self-tape.

The Self-tape Academy

At an in-person audition, there's no time to muck about. You've got to go in, deliver an awesome performance and get out again. We've all had that experience of walking back to our car after an audition, wishing we could have done another take. With self-taping, you can do the scene, review, tweak and adjust until you get it just how you want it. However, your quest to capture yourself and the scene perfectly may drive you a little crazy if you put too much pressure on yourself. It's hard, I know, to do take after take if you've already done it twenty times. Sometimes, I end up screaming at myself with frustration when my blooper reel has become longer than the actual footage. If you've got yourself into a tailspin, it can help to walk away for a while and have a breather. Then you can come back to it fresh and give it another shot.

Your agent is the best person to advise you on important tweaks to make to your self-tape before submitting. If you don't have an agent and you're submitting to an open casting, try to find someone who can give you an unbiased opinion. Friends and family will be reluctant to say anything critical, even if they promise to be honest.

What you'll need

Some people like to have all the gear when they shoot their self-tapes, from expensive cameras to lighting equipment and microphones, but remember what matters most is the acting. A sub-par performance captured with fancy equipment will not land you roles. If you have the budget, awesome; but if not, you can still do an excellent low-cost self-tape if you have set yourself up properly.

A filming space

Self-taping brings the audition process into your own environment, where you may feel more relaxed. Just don't get too relaxed and procrastinate. Find a spot with a blank white or grey wall, if you can, with no artwork or distracting features. If you don't have a blank wall to work with and you have some set-up budget, there are backdrop kits you can buy with collapsible screens. You can also just as easily use a bed sheet or curtain to create a solid colour behind you. Just ensure you clip the fabric in place so it's tight and isn't a crumpled piece of material.

A camera

If you have the budget to invest in a DSLR camera, then knock yourself out, but filming your self-tape on your phone is also perfectly acceptable. For example, iPhones have high-spec inbuilt cameras. If your phone doesn't have a great camera, you could purchase an external lens for better video quality, but of course this depends on your budget.

You can invest in a tripod and rig to get your camera right where you want it, or you might have to be inventive with some textbooks on a table. It doesn't matter how you stabilise your camera, only that it is held steady. It won't be considered an awesome audition if you had someone holding the camera, which shook the entire time, or if it was set up below eye level so we spent the entire clip looking up your nose.

Microphone

You don't have to buy a boom, but using a plug-in microphone will help capture your voice more distinctly while filtering out background noise. A lavaliere microphone that you attach to your shirt is another option if you're looking at buying some gear. The built-in microphone on your phone is likely to pick up everything, including the dog barking next door, but you might be fine if you are in a quiet location. Whatever mic you end up using, keep it out of sight so it doesn't distract the viewer.

Lighting

What's the light like in your space? The casting director needs to see the acting happening in your eyes. Natural light is best, but it sometimes needs a boost depending on the time of day and the weather. You can use a ring light, which plugs into your phone, or soft box lights if you want to get the gear (if you wear glasses, watch for reflection as that can be off-putting). Too much light will make it look like you're in front of headlights, and standing in front of a window will turn you into a dark silhouette. Play around with the light in your space and watch your recording to see if it's too dark or if the light is overpowering.

An appropriate outfit

Wearing an over-the-top costume may detract from your performance and could be problematic if you have a different visual idea of the character from the director. If you decide to wear one, commit fully and wear it confidently. When I auditioned for a horse-riding show, I wore full jodhpurs, a riding cap and had a riding crop. I looked the shit, freaking amazing. The casting director could see me as the character because I was dressed for the part. The more you become the director's vision, the easier it is for them to cast you. They know what they want, and when they see it, they book you.

Otherwise, you could choose an accessory like a hat, a jacket or glasses to help you embody the character. You might wear something that hints at the character's appearance. For example, if your character is a businessperson, you might wear a plain collared shirt instead of a full suit and tie. Avoid wearing anything overly baggy. The casting team wants to see your body shape.

Props and set items

Build up a collection of props to use if the scene calls for it, but be appropriate with them. If the scene mentions a phone, use a phone. Don't grab a book and tap on it, pretending it's a phone. You don't need to carry a sword or a briefcase unless the scene directs you to do something with them. Otherwise, these props are likely to confuse the scene rather than add to it. Make your environment as realistic as possible. If it's an office scene, don't shoot it in your bathroom; set up a desk and a laptop.

A good reader

Unless you're recording a monologue, you'll need a reader to say your lines to. Because you're doing a self-tape, you're in complete control of who you pick to be your reader, which is an advantage over an in-person audition. You can take this chance to choose a reader who will help you shine, preferably another actor who understands the role of a reader. You can ask them to adjust their delivery to work with yours, such as the timing of their lines.

If you're on a tight deadline and you have nobody to be your reader, you could record yourself saying the other character's lines and play it in the background. Do not attempt to act both sides of the scene, and never say your lines to the camera instead of a reader.

By offering to be a reader for other actors (check out the Actor Trade app), you can build on your knowledge and experience of self-taping. Also, reading for others will hopefully connect you to enough actors who will return the favour.

Editing software

There is editing software on most smartphones, such as iMovie or Windows Movie Maker. You could also purchase professional software programmes, like Cap Cut, but there are plenty of free or low-cost editing software offerings online that should meet the needs of a self-tape edit. There are a lot of tutorials on YouTube to help you work out how to use these programmes.

Editing Software

Nailing your self-tape audition

You might have the best equipment and the perfect set up, but how well you deliver the requested scenes will be what makes the difference. Let's walk through a few things that will help you capture yourself in the best light possible.

Remove all distractions

If you have a few flatmates, you might want to ask them nicely to head out for a few hours so you can get your self-tape done, and for the love of God, remove your cat or dog from the area. If the casting director's eye is drawn away from you while you are speaking, you've lost them. Closing your doors and windows will hopefully keep environmental noises low.

Follow the instructions

Self-tape auditions generally have specific instructions. Read them and follow them. This will put you in a good light. It can be so frustrating when you ask an actor to do something specific for their self-tape and they don't. I had a casting brief come across my desk looking for young male actors who could sing and play the guitar. I asked a couple of my clients with those skills to send me a self-tape of them singing while playing a guitar. One sent me a tape of themselves singing with no guitar and the other one sent me a tape of them playing the guitar without singing. I wanted to pull my hair out. I had to go back to them and ask them to kindly read my instructions again and resubmit.

So, pay close attention to what's being asked of you. For example, sometimes you might be asked for different takes of the same scene, conveying different emotions. Or they might ask you to do multiple clips showing the different sides of a dialogue.

Did they ask you to slate at the beginning of your tape? This is when you stand in front of the camera and say your name and other details, like your height and the name of your agent. Some people don't slate unless specifically asked, but I always slate because there can be hundreds of submissions for a role. It's important they have your information. Check the instructions to see if they asked for any specific information, like what part of the country you're from.

There will probably be instructions that cover how they'd like you to send the footage. For example, what file type do they want, e.g., MP4, MOV, etc. You may need to compress your file before sending, so check the file size. Did they ask you to upload it via their own online portal or via a private link on Vimeo or YouTube?

Direct your reader

Grabbing your flatmate to be your reader could sink your audition unless you give them proper direction. They should be to the left or right of the camera and not in the shot so you don't confuse the casting director regarding whose audition it is. Since they are usually closer to the camera than you, they will probably need to lower their volume, but they don't need to whisper. The casting director needs to hear both sides of the dialogue clearly for the scene to work. Plus, if they are too far from the camera, you will turn your head to talk to them, and we will only see your profile; we won't see the acting happening in your eyes.

I had to do a self-tape where my reader was saying the lines for four different scene partners. They stood in one place, and I marked my environment with objects (like pot plants and bags) to ensure I looked in the right direction when saying my lines. It was no small task to try to remember which objects were saying what lines. I think I must have done twenty takes!

If they are reading the lines of multiple characters (like mine was), they don't have to change their voice to suit. The casting director just needs someone to fill the dialogue; they are looking at your acting in response to it. If the reader started doing different voices, it would be very distracting. This may seem like a silly thing to have to say, but as a casting director I've seen it all, including readers who have read the stage directions aloud.

Shoot in landscape

Generally, auditions are taped in landscape. Things are changing these days with Tiktok, YouTube shorts and Instagram IGTV/reels, which are set up for portrait video, but movie screens, TVs and laptops are still landscape, and that's what your audition is likely to be viewed on. You don't want your footage to look stretched or tiny on the screen, so follow the standard advice and shoot in landscape.

Whether you shoot the footage as a mid-shot or close up really depends on the scene. If the scene involves you talking to a crowd of people, then it would make sense to use a mid-shot so the camera can capture your arm gestures and the context of the situation. But if it is a dramatic scene with a lot of emotion or intensity, you'd want to do a close-up so the casting director can see your facial expressions. Over-the-top facial expressions are not necessary. When you are truly embodying the emotion you're expressing, you won't need to be over the top to get your point across. It will radiate from you.

Moving too much in a close-up shot puts you in danger of moving out of frame or going out of focus. You could put a tape mark on the floor so you remain conscious of the space you can move within. Don't do any strange camera angles or try panning. Just keep it still and at eye level. The casting director wants to see your acting skills, not fancy camera work.

Be bold

A bold decision can be your downfall or get you a callback. I made that decision to wear full horse-riding gear despite general industry advice erring on the side of caution when it comes to wearing costumes. Sometimes, you've got to take a risk.

A true example of bold choices is Dacre Montgomery's self-tape audition for *Stranger Things*. He broke many of the conventional rules, such as slating in character, wearing no shirt and doing a transition clip, but he did it so confidently and acted so well, it served him.[70]

Dacre Montgomery's Self-Tape

Another person who took a risk with their self-tape audition was Austin Butler, who filmed himself singing and playing *Unchained Melody* on the piano for the role of Elvis. He'd just woken up, his hair was a mess and he was in his bathrobe. He shared what happened in an interview with *The Project*: 'I woke up in an awful place, and I thought, "What would Elvis do with this?" He would put it all into music.'[71]

Austin Butler's Interview

70 GQ. (2017, November 3). *Stranger Things' Dacre Montgomery's Insane 'Billy' Audition Tape | GQ* [Video].
71 The Project. (2022, June 5). *Austin Butler On How Auditioning In A Bathrobe Made Him A King* [Video].

If this inspires you to do something rebellious, let me offer you a word of caution. If you're going to break the rules, please understand this could put you on the 'no' pile straight away. It won't always work in your favour like it did for Dacre and Austin. That's what makes it a risk.

Memorise your lines

You know what I'm going to say here, and I'm going to say it again. Learn your lines. Learn them inside out, upside down and backwards. Why? Because you want to be off book for your self-tape audition, and by off book, I mean no script in hand because you have your lines memorised.

The minute we can see that you're trying to remember the lines in your head, you become unbelievable. People do not look up into their heads unless they're trying to remember something. They also don't randomly glance down or away from the person they're talking to in order to read their next line.

Actors try all sorts of tricks that casting directors can see straight through. Some try taping the words next to the camera, others get the reader to hold up the lines in front of them. Whatever trick you try, I assure you WE CAN TELL. And it's not just that we can tell you're reading, it's that you've paused your character. Even if it's a quick pause, you go out of character to read the lines. If you are truly in character, there are no lines, because acting is making us believe the dialogue is real.

If it's a tight deadline, most casting directors will be okay with some paraphrasing, but be sure you don't change the context of the story. How you say a line can be very important. There are countless ways to say the same sentence. You can say 'I love you' with a sarcastic tone, with a desperate tone or with a humorous tone. It's important you understand the scene and what kind of tone you should use.

If acting is truly what you want to do, then I encourage you to take self-taping seriously. This is a legitimate auditioning process used more widely now than ever before. Learning the ins and outs of what's required to self-tape and practising putting one together will strengthen your ability to memorise scripts and feel confident in front of a camera, two things you'll need when you head to your in-person auditions.

CHAPTER NINETEEN

Auditions

People may tell you that auditions get easier over time, but that's never been the case for me. I have always found them nerve-racking, even when I personally know the casting director; actually, ESPECIALLY if I know the casting director. I'd much rather audition for someone I don't know.

Most actors, even the famous ones, dread auditions. But if you want to be an actor, then going to auditions is like going to work. A cashier at the supermarket beeps groceries through the checkout, and that's what they do, beep, beep, beep. Actors go to auditions, they audition and audition and audition, and that's what they do until they land a role, and then they go back to auditioning.

Preparing for your audition

If you don't take your auditions seriously, you'll soon get a name for yourself as a time waster. That's when the auditions dry up, and you know you're really in trouble. So, let's get serious and start by looking at things you can do to make the process easier.

Be early

You'd be surprised how many actors fail this first task. Consider travel time, parking, and finding the location; you don't want to be turning up looking like a frazzled mess. You'll also need to leave time for filling out forms on arrival, and sometimes there's a tape measure on the wall for you to check your height. Don't guess if the ability to check it is there. Height can be very important for some roles. Be honest about your body measurements. Lying will get you nowhere fast.

Shhhhh

People are shooting auditions, and the casting team doesn't want to hear a garble of chitchat from the waiting room. Also, your fellow actors may be trying to 'get in the zone', so maybe you should do the same?

Should you bring a prop(s)?

You could, and having a prop may indeed make you stand out from the other actors. If the scene has specific actions in it, like drinking from a glass, the glass should be provided, but if you're thinking that your character would hold or carry something, then sure, bring it along and go for it. Keep in mind, however, that there are risks in choosing to bring a prop along. The director may have a completely different vision of your character than you do, so your prop idea may not align with what they have in their head. Also, a prop can sometimes be distracting. I once brought along a notebook and pen to an audition because, in my mind, my character was writing while she was talking. However, writing while I was auditioning meant I had my head down a lot, and they couldn't see the acting happening in my face. When I realised this, I kept looking up to ensure they could see me, but it was all a bit inauthentic. My character had no reason to keep looking up. In the end, I tried acting with a prop. It didn't work out, but at least I learned something.

Get into character

While you are waiting to audition, you can use this time to connect deeply with your character. How would they act in a waiting room? What would they do if they were feeling nervous? See if you can relate to the same feelings your character would have at this moment. In that way, when you step into the audition room, you'll already have them with you.

Getting your voice ready

We covered the benefit of vocal warmups and looking after your voice in chapter ten, 'Develop Some Special Skills.' That was in regards to learning to sing, but if you're not taking singing lessons and you don't have a vocal coach, you can still look up some vocal warmup exercises to do before your audition. Personally, I used to think doing vocal warmups was a waste of time, but I've come to understand that warming up your vocals lets you speak with greater strength, depth and control.

Try to find a private spot when you arrive at your audition so you can do your vocal warmups without disrupting anyone. Alternatively, do them in your car or outside. Here are a couple of warmups I suggest:

Yawning

Doing a couple of yawns while making a high to low sigh can help to relax the jaw. If you're around other people, you could just massage your jaw a little, particularly your chewing muscles, where a lot of tension can get trapped.

Tongue Twisters

Mumble some tongue twisters to yourself, like 'green glass grass gleams' or 'a regal rural ruler'. You might think they're silly, but you won't be laughing if you keep tripping over your lines again and again because you haven't limbered up your tongue.

Face yoga

Yes, it's a thing. Facial expressions are a huge part of acting, so it shouldn't surprise you that exercises have been created specifically for loosening up the facial muscles to allow for greater expression.

Breath work

The 4–7–8 breath exercise is when you inhale for four counts, hold for seven and then breathe out for eight.[72] Focus on breathing all the way down your stomach. This exercise is both calming and great for helping you have better control of your breath while speaking.

---

72 Pichardo, G. (2023, June 27). *What to Know About 4-7-8 Breathing*. WebMD.

It's normal to be nervous

Despite my many years of experience, I still suffer from imposter syndrome now and then. I've come to realise that this type of anxiety is common amongst actors, even big movie stars. In a way, that little bit of doubt (or large bit) keeps you moving towards improvement. When you start thinking you've nailed every audition, you've closed the door on the chance to learn more, and there's always something new to learn in the big wide world of acting.

Keep in mind that a little bit of nervous energy is reasonable. It means that your work is important to you and you're not smug about your abilities. But if it really worries you, take a stroll back to chapter eight, 'Do Some Amateur Theatre', where I gave a few tips for calming your nerves.

Remember, if you're worrying about whether you will get the part before you've even done the audition, you're too far ahead in your thinking. Just concentrate on the audition; there'll be plenty of time to worry about whether you've got it or not afterwards.

Theatre auditions

Theatre encompasses a range of productions, from musicals to operas and comedies, so the structure of their auditions and their requirements will differ. If it's a big budget stage production looking for professional actors, the audition script will come to you via your agent. Local amateur dramatic productions will give you the chance to audition for several roles, with specific audition days for each part in the play.

For musical productions, your audition will include a song, and in fact, may only be a song. They may assign the song or ask you to choose one.

If you have been asked to choose one, bring the sheet music with you and hand it to the accompanist on arrival. Make sure you point out any notes regarding key changes or tempo. If casting has assigned a song that includes notes that fall outside your vocal range, you may be able to transpose the music into a different key. It is better to do this than try to hit notes you can't usually hit.

Theatre productions that are less musical in nature will generally have their actors perform a monologue, which we covered in chapter twelve. The monologue scene will be sent to your agent, and you should try to get off book as soon as possible. When you're performing, focus all your attention on your scene partner, whether that's a reader or a light stand you've chosen to represent the other character. Doing so will help you project your performance and be less conscious of yourself.

Commercial auditions

Before you go to a commercial audition, do a bit of research on the product or service the advertisement is selling. What is the look and feel of the brand? Present yourself accordingly.

Compared to television and movie auditions, commercials tend to be quick. You either fit the brief or you don't. This doesn't mean your delivery should be rushed. Take the time to say the lines as intended. The casting director will usually do a run through / rehearsal first, and they may even shoot it. Listen carefully to feedback and adjust your delivery to suit. Hopefully, you've been playing with different deliveries, so you haven't got yourself stuck and unable to change it up.

Once you're done, the casting director will know immediately whether they want you to do another take or if they want to send you on your way. If you did only two takes, you either smashed it straight off the bat or, unfortunately, you didn't get the part. If the casting director is getting you to do several takes, it's likely they like what they see and want to have various options for the director to view.

Television and movie auditions

Your agent will be sent sides of a scene for your TV or movie audition. They may be random scenes from existing television shows or movies in order to protect the plot. Television and movie productions go to great lengths to maintain a shroud of secrecy around plotlines and casting. The cast of *Stranger Things*, for example, were sent scenes from the movie *Stand by Me* for their auditions.[73] Once filming starts, productions continue to protect the plot. The Marvel franchise went as far to giving their cast fake scripts to avoid accidental spoilers.

Fake Scripts from Marvel

You may also be given a character description, which will help you connect with the role. You need to spend your audition prep time not only learning the lines but really getting to know your character. If the description is short and not in depth, flesh your character out yourself using a character development template. Think about who you're playing. Are they from a particular place and time? What was happening

73 Mink, C. (2021, January 8). *How 'Stranger Things' Got Made.* Backstage.

in that era? You want to be a believable character, and real people reflect a past, place and era in their personality. You might never be asked to act in a way that shows the true depth of the character you've created, but you will hold that depth within you when you stand in front of the casting director.

Character Development Template

When you enter the audition space, there will be a reader who will sit to the left or the right of the camera. If there are multiple people in a scene, there might be multiple readers, or they may bring in other actors whom they want you to audition with. They might get a whole group of you in to see how you blend, or they might swap and switch people around to see how you match with different people.

For any audition being filmed (that means commercials, television or movies), you will enter a room and stand on an 'X' marked on the floor, where you'll do your slate (introducing yourself). Most of the time, you will hold up to the camera a board that will have your information written on it, such as your name and agent/agency. They'll take a picture of you, and then they may ask you if you're available for specific shoot dates as well as any other important information they need to capture. You'll turn to the side and sometimes to the back so the camera can capture your body shape. Kind of like a prison mug shot.

After this, you will act out the audition scene in a space that's been set up near the slate spot. Your take on the scene and your character's personality may not be exactly what they're looking for, so be ready for direction. Do your best and don't let your nerves stuff up your listening skills.

If you think the audition went well and the vibe feels good, you could take the chance to offer yourself as a reader for the casting director. No doubt almost every actor that came through the door made the same offer, but that doesn't mean you shouldn't throw your hat in the ring. Being a reader at auditions is a great way to build a relationship with casting directors, and readers are sometimes cast in the productions they read for, so even though you may not get paid for your time, the effort you put in could well pay off in its own way.

Cold readings

Sometimes, casting will give actors scenes to read through with very little time to prepare. You might be given as little as thirty minutes before being called in. There are a few reasons why cold reads are used. Sometimes, you'll audition for a particular part, and the casting team may think you're potentially a good fit for a different part. They'll give you a different script and ask you to come back in an hour, for example, and audition for that part instead. Other times, you might audition for a commercial and the advertising team changes the script the night before.

All you can do is try your best in these situations, but there is one thing I suggest regarding cold readings. Scan the script and look for THE pivotal moment. This scene has been chosen for the audition because something important happens in it. It won't be a scene of two people talking about the weather. Find that moment where the scene changes in emotion and intensity. That's the part you need to nail. Find it and memorise it as best you can. The casting team is looking closely at that moment where your character must change their stance, and they want to see how well you pull that off. Cold readings are loathed by actors, but ultimately, it is a chance to show them how quick you are on your feet. Embrace it.

A callback tale

The character I auditioned for in *Top of the Lake* had nude scenes in the show. I was aware of that going into my first audition, but I knew that only the actors called back for a second audition would need to do a nude scene, and at that point, a callback was far from my mind.

And then it happened. I got the callback. I was excited and equally terrified. I thought I might explode. On the day of the callback, I turned up super early and sat in my car, nearly smoking myself to death, trying to calm my nerves. I watched A-class actors coming and going from the audition rooms whilst I sat in my car waiting to go in. I thought to myself, 'Oh my God, how am I going to live up to that? I'm just Sarah Valentine. They're never going to pick me.' I was extremely nervous, but the casting director was amazing. She helped me to feel safe and comfortable. The end result was me landing a role on Jane Campion's TV series, which was an unforgettable experience and worth every second I stood starkers in front of her.

Lessons learned from my time as a casting director

It was always important to me, as a casting director, that I do my best to make everyone feel relaxed, because I knew, as an actor myself, what it's like to walk into an audition room with all those nerves. I appreciated actors who allowed themselves to be vulnerable in front of me, because I know how hard that can be.

I've seen the best of the best and the worst of the worst in regards to auditions. One of my most trying experiences was when I was looking for a female lead and the audition scene was extremely emotional. The character came home and found out their child had died. You can only imagine, I bet, what a traumatic day that was for all of us. For the entire day, I had these women screaming and crying in front of me. Some were so believable, I felt like I was witnessing the experience for real. Others were completely over acting and being crazy to the point that I would run and hide so I didn't laugh in front of them. You never want to hurt someone's feelings, but boy, oh boy! Sometimes you are biting your lip! I felt like I was inside a bad B-grade horror film and I couldn't escape.

Thankfully, my time as a casting director wasn't all bad acting and holding my head in my hands. I've seen some amazing auditions; real magic. When you see the actor being taken over by the character, you're transported by their performance. When you've got that gold from an actor, you know it.

When an actor comes in and they know the lines, they have the story in their eyes and they're completely believable, it's a wonderful feeling. All your senses are electric, and there's just this fizz of energy in the room. Everything just melts away and an entirely different reality unfolds. It would take my breath away, and I would think, 'That's it, that's acting.'

So, from my experience, what would I say to hopeful actors wanting to make the best possible impression at their audition?

Learn your lines

I don't care how many times I've already said it, I will say it till the cows come home: please, learn your lines. *Learn them inside out, upside down and backwards, know them off by heart!* Don't think you can look at the script a few times and just wing it. A casting director's job is to get a great performance out of an actor, but if you don't know your lines, you don't know what you're doing, you don't look real and you're not prepared, you're wasting their time and you're not going to get the part.

Understand your scene

If you've never been in a similar situation to the scene you're about to do, you have some work to do. You might read or watch real-life or fictional stories of a similar nature so you can sift through a variety of reactions and decide which way your character would lean. For example, if you're going to be doing a scene where your wife has lost her baby, do some mental and physical prep work to be convincing in that scene.

Don't make excuses

Don't turn up to an audition bleating about traffic, your sick dog or your splitting headache. When actors do that, I know they're trying to explain away their piss-poor performance before they've even auditioned. Come in and give it all you've got, or don't waste my time.

Auditioning is a mixed bag of experiences. You will have wonderful auditions, and you'll also have the other kind. When your audition goes to pieces, you may feel like you want to find a rock to crawl under. I've certainly had that experience of sitting in my car afterwards thinking, 'God, can the earth just please swallow me whole right now? That was a nightmare!' And yet we keep coming back again and again, suckers for punishment.

Ryan Gosling Interview

But there are ways to cope in a cycle of rejection. I've found some great tools that help me, and I'll share them with you in the chapter ahead, 'Dealing with Rejection'.

CHAPTER TWENTY

Dealing with Rejection

For many, many years, I would leave an audition, sit by the phone and wait. Have I got it? Have I got it? No, I haven't got it. That would be my pattern again and again. The hoping and waiting were torture. I once had to wait three months to hear if I had landed a role, and I can tell you it was three months of agony.

The problem was that I was pinning my self-worth to the success of my auditions. It was a recipe for disaster, since actors only ever land a small portion of roles they audition for. I was setting myself up for devastation again and again. Eventually, I realised that taking each rejection to heart was reducing me to nothing. I had to change my outlook, mindset and approach. Ahead, I'll share a few techniques I use that might help you learn to live with the rejection that comes hand in hand with this industry.

See auditioning as a job

About 10–15 years ago, I decided to stop equating my value with my ability to land roles. Instead, I started treating each audition as a separate job. I'd practise my lines, give it 100% and leave; job done. In my view, I'd accomplished my task and there was no rejection involved.

It's not that I'm indifferent to the process; of course, I want the parts I audition for. But I have found this approach lets me feel free and empowered after each audition without enduring an emotional rollercoaster. I could tick the auditions off as complete in my mind instead of waiting nervously for a phone call that never comes. In a nutshell, I separated myself from the outcome, and I'll admit it's hard to do, because of course you want the role.

If they rang me afterwards to say 'We really liked your audition, we'd like you to come in for a callback', then I would count that as the beginning of a new job. I become a little bit more invested emotionally at this point because I know I have a greater chance of getting the part. Generally, they don't call to let you know you didn't get it, but sometimes you'll receive an email that says, 'This role has now been cast'. By that time, I've moved on, because I let the job go once the audition is over (well, I try to, anyway).

After the audition

I don't recommend going home to pace your living room and replay the audition over and over in your head. Organising to meet up with a friend or family member might be a good idea, especially if they're a good listener. You might need to unpack how it went, you might need to cry or vent or you might need to toast a really awesome audition. Either way, good company will replenish you and help you feel supported. If you don't think it went well, here are some things you can do to help move on:

It's not always about your acting

There are many, many reasons why an actor isn't cast, and it can have nothing to do with how well or how poorly you performed. This industry is fickle. It can come down to factors beyond your control, like your height or facial features. You might absolutely nail the audition to find out later that the part went to the director's nephew. Nepotism is part of show business, I'm afraid, and this is definitely an industry where people use their connections to get ahead.

If I don't get a part, I'm always curious to watch the movie or show when it comes out to see who did. Usually, I can see immediately why I didn't get it and why I wasn't what they were looking for. In your head, you were perfect for the role, but the director knows what they are looking for, and their vision may be different from yours. It's their prerogative to go after what they want.

Express your feelings, but don't wallow

Trying to ignore or push down negative feelings can be unhealthy. If it sucked, it sucked, and your feelings are valid. You're disappointed because you're passionate, and that's a good thing. Find a healthy way to let your feelings out, and then let them go. Don't get on social media and badmouth a casting director or other actors; that will certainly not help your career. If you need to hit the gym and punch a punching bag, do it. Be careful not to be swallowed by your feelings, though. A cry in the shower is one thing; being stuck in bed for days is another. You can't afford to crumble completely after each audition; you need to pick yourself back up and get on with the next one.

Be honest with yourself

We all make mistakes. The important thing is to acknowledge them, accept that you made them (instead of making excuses) and resolve to learn from them. You know if you stuffed up the lines, said something inappropriate or tried to be funny and ended up being awkward. Just be honest with yourself. Was a weakness exposed during the audition? What can you do to strengthen yourself in that area?

It may feel awful now, but one day you could share what happened as a funny story on a talk show. Jake Gyllenhaal told Jimmy Fallon a hilarious story of his terrible audition for Frodo on 'Lord of the Rings', so keep in mind that even stars bomb auditions.[74]

Jake Gyllenhaal's Interview

You only see the successes

Every actor who graces Broadway, movie screens and television shows has gone through their fair share of rejection. When you see a new star in a breakout role, it's easy to think they were

---

74 The Tonight Show. (2016, March 22). *Jake Gyllenhaal Bombed His Lord of the Rings Audition* [Video]. YouTube.

lucky, but there isn't a famous actor in existence who didn't do the hard slog of auditioning and missing out before finally landing roles. In fact, some of those big stars were scarily close to quitting before they finally broke through. Melissa McCarthy told Howard Stern in an interview that she was going to quit the day she turned thirty. The day before her birthday, she got the call that she'd landed the role as Sookie on *Gilmore Girls.*[75] So, when you're feeling like you can't take any more rejection, just push yourself to do one more audition; you never know, it could be the one.

Melissa McCarthy's Interview

It's not a 'no', it's a 'not this time'

The word 'no' has such a finality to it, but there's nothing final about the world of auditions. There's always another one coming up, so it's only a 'no, not ever' if you stop going. That auditions are still coming your way means that casting teams are still willing to see you. If they really thought you were awful, you wouldn't keep getting audition opportunities, so keep turning up to get that 'yes'.

---

75 The Howard Stern Show (2019, September 16). *Melissa McCarthy Almost Quit Acting Days Before Landing 'Gilmore Girls' (2014)* [Video]. YouTube.

It's not personal, but it sure feels that way

You'll hear this again and again: a casting rejection is not personal. They don't hate you, and there are no hard feelings. But there are hard feelings on your part, aren't there? Your sadness and disappointment are personal to you. That's because this is your passion, your time, your hopes, your dream and your energy. So, perhaps the better thing to say is it's not personal to casting, but it's probably personal to you, and that's okay.

It's out of your hands

Just as you have no power over whether you are cast in a role, you also have no power over the final edit. You can give the performance of your life, but not everything filmed will make the final cut. I cried my eyes out for a particular scene with a group of actors, but my face didn't end up on screen, and that's just the way it is. There are even actors who have had their entire character and story arc removed in post-production, which must feel like a monumental waste of time for the actor.

Shailene Woodley's scenes as Mary-Jane in *The Amazing Spider-Man 2* were cut after being shot. She said in an interview with *Vanity Fair*, 'For a few hours, it was literally like, oh my God, was I awful? Why did they cut me?' Thankfully for Shailene, director Marc Webb put out a statement explaining the film needed to focus on the romantic relationship between Peter and Gwen, and that's why her character was cut.[76]

It's fair to say that most actors are unhappy when their scenes are cut. The late Christopher Lee shared his feelings of disbelief in a Q&A talk at

---

76 Gennis, S. (2014, June 12). *Shailene Woodley on Being Cut from Amazing Spiderman 2: "Was I Awful?"* TVGuide.

the University College Dublin when he learned that his scenes were cut from the *Lord of the Rings: Return of the King* movie. 'When the third film came out, I couldn't believe what I saw, because I wasn't in it.'[77] The scenes were of the death of his character, the evil wizard Saruman. If you're as upset as Christopher Lee was that his death scene was cut from the film, then you can take some solace in knowing that it does feature in the extended DVD version of the film.

Christopher Lee's Q and A

I can only imagine how frustrated actors must feel when all their hard work ends up on the cutting-room floor. I've had some of my scenes cut in the past, but they were cut before they were shot, because the director had to prioritise other character storylines over mine for the overall plot of the show. I wouldn't say that I was happy my scenes were cut before shooting (because I would have preferred they weren't cut at all), but if I had worked hard to deliver the scenes only for them to be cut afterwards, I think that would have been far worse.

Unfortunately, some actors have their scenes cut because, ultimately, they weren't very good. To be fair, it is difficult for an actor to always give a great performance, and they might have had an off day when their scenes were shot. It can also depend on the budget of the project. If your

---

77 UCD – University College Dublin (2011, November 10). *"I couldn't believe what I saw – I wasn't in it!" Christopher Lee on 'The Return of the King'* [Video]. YouTube.

show has lots of money, they'll shoot the scene until they've got it. If budgets are tight, they'll shoot and hope for the best in the editing room.

Finding ways to act without the rejection

If you can, try to keep an element of acting in your life that has no rejection attached. You could do some theatre sports/improv, join a drama club or enrol in an expressive movement class. Some actors are having fun doing 'lip sync' challenges on Tiktok. They choose a well-known scene, learn the lines and then film themselves delivering it. Some actors are duetting scenes on the platform; check them out for a few giggles and entertainment. Doing fun things like this will help keep your passion for acting alive. It's important to remind yourself why you do it, as that will keep you energised.

> For the most part, you're probably never going to know why you didn't get a role. When I was working in casting, I would try to write notes on each actor who auditioned for me, but sometimes it's impossible to give feedback to every actor who stands in front of you. On a few occasions, actors would come to an audition and ask me why they didn't get a part from a previous casting. I'd be thinking, 'Oh God, please don't ask me that'. They didn't get it because they didn't get it, and I'd much prefer they focused on the audition they're doing right now.

> Rejection is a part of being an actor, and finding ways to accept that and deal with it proactively is important. It hurts sometimes, and you may feel like giving up, but each rejection leaves you free to pursue the next opportunity, which could be the big one. So, keep your head up, because you never know, not getting that part could be the best thing that ever happened to you. When you do land a role, that's when the paperwork begins, but don't get overwhelmed. We cover contracts next.

CHAPTER
TWENTY-ONE

Contracts

You got the gig, congratulations! So what's next? The first thing to come your way will be your contract. Contracts can be heavy documents filled with lots of jargon. Thankfully, your agent can decipher everything in there and catch anything that's missing. When one of my clients was cast in a movie, I was quick to discover a clause in his contract granting permission for the studio to create a toy figurine based on his character. I was on the phone hotly to ensure he would be adequately compensated for the use of his likeness; the clause was updated appropriately. Agents know exactly what to look for when combing through a contract, and most should cover the same core components:

Your pay

Top of the list is a clear outline of how much you'll be paid, when you'll be paid and in what circumstances you wouldn't be paid. This is a crucial component of your contract, so make sure you've read and understood these terms.

Your rate

This could be per hour, per day, per week, per month, per performance or include a percentage of profits. If you are a principal actor, there may be an additional clause in your contract outlining residual payment percentages for the rerun of movies or television shows (see below).

Overtime

A normal working day on set is ten hours, but twelve-hour days are quite common. How you are paid for overtime will vary depending on your global location. In New Zealand, for example, hours eleven and twelve are generally paid at time and a half. Hours beyond twelve are usually paid at double time. Productions don't plan to work their actors overtime, but if the schedule is running tight, it can become necessary. If you are asked to work overtime, ensure you let your agent know, so they can invoice for the correct number of hours at the right rate.

'Pay or play' vs 'run of play'

The term 'pay or play' is used in contracts to ensure an actor will be paid their negotiated fee, whether they are used in the final film / TV show or not. It ensures an actor gets their compensation either way, and it allows directors and/or producers to replace an actor or remove them without threat of legal retribution by the actor. 'Run of Play' is a similar term used in theatre contracts. It ensures an actor is paid for the length or 'run' of a show/production if they, too, are replaced or removed. Both of these terms are used with exceptions, such as an instance where an actor is in breach of contract or the production is halted due to 'an act of God'.

Residuals

This is payment for work you've already done in a film, commercial or TV show that is rerun or redistributed at a later date. The details of the residuals, such as how much you'll receive and for how long, can be different in each country. It may depend on union agreements or on what your agent negotiates for you. Not all jobs will include residuals, but it's worth negotiating to receive them if you can.

Your time

Time is money, and your time is just as precious as theirs. It's important to know what the production's expectations are around working on other projects and how they will compensate you for working long hours.

Ongoing Commitment

For a pilot TV show, your contract will probably require that you commit to working for a predetermined period if the show is picked up by a network. This could be a long-term agreement, possibly years, so be sure you want to be tied to this project before signing. There could be legal ramifications if you change your mind.

Availability

Your contract should outline what dates you will be available for filming and the main locations, e.g., June 1–30, London. The contract won't specify which days within that date range you will be required for filming. That comes later when you receive your DOOD, 'Day Out Of Days', which will have all the dates listed.

Against your name will be a date that has 'SW' (start work), which is your first day. There will be a number of dates with 'W' (work) and finally you'll see 'WF' (work finish) for your last day.

When you're starting out, it can feel like a big ask to keep yourself available for a whole week when you might be scheduled only to be on set for one day. Later on in your career, you could negotiate for compensation for your availability. You don't have to sit at home during your available days; just be strategic. Schedule your work around your filming days and be ready and willing to get to set if needed. Generally, your DOOD will not change, because rearranging filming days can cause a lot of disruption, especially if locations have been booked. However, things happen. People get sick, family members pass away, weather events occur.

For theatre, the contract will include your rehearsal schedule as well as the performance dates and the details of any tours.

Breaking turnaround

A ten-hour break between shooting times is required for actors, which is called 'turnaround'. However, productions sometimes need to break turnaround to stay on schedule. The penalties for breaking turnaround are quite costly since everyone staying will be paid overtime. Productions try to avoid doing it, but sometimes the deadline is more important than the money.

Exclusivity

Some contracts prohibit actors from taking part in other work while they are employed on a project, and sometimes the period of exclusivity can extend for a period beyond the premiere of the film, TV show or closing of the production.

During filming/show dates

You need to be taken care of during shoots and stage tours. Contracts should carefully outline all the provisions that will be made for you:

Travel arrangements

If you are filming at a location far away from where you live or touring with a stage show, your contract should outline what travel arrangements will be made for you, plus your accommodation if required. If these are not booked for you, the contract should confirm an allowance or per diem that will cover the cost of your travel, meals and accommodation.

Your gig may not require you to travel to a location, but if it does, your contract will outline what days you are to arrive and depart. While on location, you need to stay put. All your food and accommodation requirements will be met, and even though you might find yourself with downtime, you need to remain at the ready. I was once in a remote location filming and had to miss a dear friend's wedding. It was hugely disappointing considering I wasn't needed for filming at all on the day, but the fact of the matter is that I'd signed a contract to be on site during a specific time frame, and although I wasn't needed, schedules can change and scenes can get swapped around.

Meal breaks

Though you would expect to be fed and watered while on set, it is important this is confirmed in the contract. Filming can mean long days, and so by law meal breaks should be provided, and since they are unlikely to want you leaving the set, they should provide food onsite. You may be asked to have a 'running lunch' (where you eat on set instead of going to the designated eating spot). This is something actors are compensated for.

In theatre, food is sometimes provided in the green room or other designated areas, but generally actors are given enough time for their meal breaks to go and get food offsite. The difference is studios and filming locations are usually some distance from food offerings, while theatres are more centralised with eateries nearby. Also, some theatres do not allow any food or drink in their space.

Wardrobe

Generally your costumes and wardrobe are arranged by the production, but some actors are asked to wear their own clothes, in which case there may be a clause offering replacement costs if they are damaged and dry cleaning post use. Some actors negotiate an agreement to keep their wardrobe after wrapping. Reece Witherspoon famously arranged in her contract to keep her entire costume wardrobe from *Legally Blonde 2*, which included 77 pairs of Jimmy Choo shoes.[78]

Reece Witherspoon Interview

---

78 The Graham Norton Show (2019, November 2). *"What Jennifer Aniston, Reece Witherspoon & Dame Julie Andrews Stole from Sets* [Video]. YouTube.

Specific expectations

This includes any expectations that the actor will do tasks over and above normal acting requirements, such as stunts or nude scenes. For nudity, contracts should confirm a closed set, and it should be specified what kind of nudity will be required, e.g., upper body exposed, lower half from behind, etc. Some actors negotiate for a body double to be used when it comes to nudity or body-specific shots.

Legal

It's not the most exciting part of a contract, but it is hugely important that actors and their employers agree what it is expected from them in a legal sense. Make sure you have your head wrapped around these parts so you don't land in hot water.

Perpetuity

Definitely watch out for this word in your contract. Signing away the use of your image in perpetuity grants your employer permission to use it forever for no further compensation.

Confidentiality

Shows, films and productions don't want any leaks of rehearsals, casting or plotlines. The secrecy around some productions is a big deal, so ensure you keep your lips sealed. Mark Ruffalo and Tom Holland have become well known amongst their Marvel cast for accidentally dropping spoilers during media appearances, landing them in all sorts of trouble.[79]

---

79 Good Morning America (2017, July 19). *"Did Mark Ruffalo Accidentally Reveal*

Mark Ruffalo Interview

It is also expected that film crews will not leak information to the media, such as any difficulties or conflicts actors may have had on set. Recordings of actor outbursts are one such type of leak that can be embarrassing for an actor. Both Christian Bale and Tom Cruise have had such leaks released to the media, and many actors have come to their defence regarding the intense pressure actors can be under.[80]

Leaked Audio Interview

Clear procedures in case of a breach

For both parties, it's best that it's clearly laid out what the process

---

That Everyone Dies In Avengers Infinity War? [Video]. YouTube.
80 Associated Press (2009, May 11). *Bale Apologizes for Angry Rant* [Video]. YouTube.

will be if either party finds themselves in breach of contract. This could include fines or more serious penalties.

Post-production

Once filming wraps or the production closes, there can still be ongoing work, such as media appearances and promotional aspects.

Credit

Ensure the contract confirms you will be credited for your work and how.

Merchandise

Studios or productions may want to use your likeness for advertising or on t-shirts or even to create toys. Before you sign away permission for them to do this, you'll want to ensure you are compensated fairly.

Media and public appearances

You may be expected, as part of your contract, to attend red-carpet events. You might like to negotiate tickets to these events for friends and family. If you are in a stage production, you could also negotiate tickets to the show for friends and family to attend. Your employer may also want you to go on talk shows or give radio interviews as part of a busy post-production schedule, so have a discussion with your agent about what you're okay with.

This is not an exhaustive list, and particular projects may have specific clauses that pertain to the unique nature of the role. If there's anything missing in your contract that you think should be in there, talk it over with your agent.

Each country runs things a little differently in terms of industry standards, law requirements and union/non-union agreements. Actors who belong to a union cannot accept non-union work and will be presented with a union contract. Non-union actors can still sign a contract with a studio or theatre company, but it will be a generic industry standard agreement. Thankfully, agents can represent union and non-union actors, so either way, they can help steer you through the process. If you are unclear about unions and their purpose, you're in luck; we are covering that topic next.

CHAPTER TWENTY-TWO

Joining a Union

H eads up, this is not going to be an exciting read. However, just because unions are not the most fun part of the acting industry, that doesn't mean they are not worth writing about. It's a common question among actors: Should I join a union and why? Below, I'll give you a quick summary so you are not bored to tears but informed just the same.

Join or don't join?

This is what actors most want to know, and the answer is… that depends. The rules, regulations and benefits of joining an actors' union vary from country to country. It's important that you look up the actors' union(s) in your location and understand the specifics of their eligibility criteria and the rules of their membership. Does your union require you to only accept union roles after joining? What eligibility criteria do they have? What are the financial costs of their membership? What are the specific benefits that your union provides? Let's explore.

Sarah Valentine

Unions around the World

Are you eligible?

Some unions are harder to gain eligibility for than others. You may need to do a certain number of jobs on a union production or simply be able to provide proof of payment for work already completed. Restrictions have reduced over the years. In 2023, the Equity Union in America made their Open Access policy permanent to address inequality issues.[81]

The United Kingdom addressed access issues in the 1980s by making closed-shop unions illegal and easing criteria to join a union.[82] The closed-shop arrangement meant that you had to have acting credits to join the union, and you couldn't get much acting work without belonging to the union. When I was studying and living in the UK, I had a friend who belonged to the Equity Union and I was so jealous. She managed to get her Equity card by performing at a place called Butlin's, which was a holiday camp (think *Hi-de-Hi!*). I desperately wanted to have one just like her. Years later, when I moved to New Zealand, I

---

81 Open Access Extension/EMC Phase Out Frequently Asked Questions. Actors Equity.
82 Wintour, P. (2020, December 18). *Labour abandons the closed shop – archive, 1989* The Guardian.

found out that you could join the Equity Union there without any acting credits, so I signed up quick smart. Once I'd done that, I contacted the Equity Union in the United Kingdom and asked if I could get a card from them too, and boom! I finally realised my dream and got my British Equity card.

Are you ready to join?

Some unions require you to only accept union work in order to keep your membership. This is not true of all unions. For example, in Australia and New Zealand, there is no such thing as union and non-union work, so joining one does not restrict your employment opportunities.

For countries that do have this restriction, like America and the United Kingdom, it's important to remember that non-union work can help you gain the experience you need to improve as an actor. You'll need to consider whether you're ready to step away from non-union work completely and compete mostly with unionised actors for roles.

Can you afford it?

Take the time to check if the union(s) in your part of the world has a joining fee and what their annual dues are. Some unions require their joining fee to be paid within a certain time period from becoming eligible. Other unions allow you to pay your joining fee off over a number of years. Annual fees vary in cost and have various structures; some are determined by your annual gross income, others have different levels of membership, from background performers to full members. There are some unions that provide discounts for students, senior citizens or actors with disabilities. It really is a mixed bag out there in terms of what you can expect to pay, so this is certainly something you should take into consideration.

The benefits of joining a union

Before the invention of unions, many actors were the victims of exploitation, with some studios treating them like property. Actors were presented with long-term exclusive contracts that blocked them from opportunities, and any objections raised resulted in some being blacklisted.[83] Creatives have a long history of being exploited for their craft, and some struggle to this day to be fully recognised and properly compensated for their work. Unions exist to ensure actors are recognised for their talent and paid fairly.

Hopefully, you will always be offered fair contracts and treated well by your employer, but if you ever find you are not, being a union member usually gives you access to support, advice and advocacy. Each union will have their own list of support services they offer, such as insurance, pensions, legal advice, various discounts and healthcare plans. For the most part, unions cannot work on your behalf if you have already signed an employment contract before you joined them, but they will still do what they can to point you in the right direction.

It is a personal choice for every actor whether to join their local union. Remember that their purpose is to help actors have a voice in negotiations and fight against discrimination and unfair treatment. Many of the standard working terms and conditions actors enjoy today have been put in place through the hard work of union negotiations. From meal breaks to travel

---

83 "Screen Actors Guild." International Directory of Companies Histories. Retrieved November 15, 2023 from Encyclopedia.com.

allowances and minimum pay rates, it can be easy to take for granted provisions that were once non-existent. Unions have had varying success when it comes to their lobbying power, but at the heart of their existence is a commitment to uphold the rights of actors as professional workers. Actor unions around the world have done what they can to secure fair pay, safe working conditions and legal recourse for any breaches of contract for actors. With these safeguards in place, you can put all your focus on preparing for your role.

CHAPTER TWENTY-THREE

Pre-production

Pre-production is the period of time within which every task that needs to be completed before filming or opening night is scheduled and carried out. The tasks can be practical, like costume fittings, but can also involve deeper work, like character development and team bonding.

Ahead of filming *Top of the Lake*, director Jane Campion organised for us to arrive on location so we could help build the set and get a sense of ownership over the environment. She understood deeply the importance of setting. The remote lake location was like another character in the story. By connecting to the scenery, the set, our costumes and the props, she helped us to embody our characters more deeply than if we had arrived at a pre-built set. We created the space we worked in, and it felt like it was ours.

How long is the pre-production period?

In terms of length, pre-production periods can vary. Determining factors include the type of production and the budget. Commercials, for example, are likely to have a shorter pre-production schedule than other production types unless it is a big-budget commercial with a big-name director. Film and television pre-production schedules can be anywhere from three to seven months, but these timeframes can blow out if there are delays and if the budget allows. To try to minimise pre-production time, a lot of tasks are done simultaneously. Scouts will be out booking film locations while the crew is being hired. Pre-production for theatre is a time of intense rehearsals that can last from six to eight weeks.

During pre-production

During pre-production, you should be contacted by the cast coordinator, who is the person in charge of on-boarding the actors. They will tell you all you need to know in advance of filming and what tasks you need to complete. These could include:

Costume fittings

This is usually one of your first tasks after being cast in any production. You should be contacted and advised where to go for your measurements to be taken. There may be a second fitting to see if the costume fits as per the measurements. Sometimes, wigs have their own fitting. Get to know the people in the costume department and respect their work; they know what they're doing and aren't looking for your critique on their creation. The costume designer may photograph you and discuss the photos with the director. Television and film productions may require you to do a camera test so the cinematographer can see how the colours and textures of your clothing look in different lighting and on a big screen.

Training

Pre-production is the time during which you will learn any special skills required for your role, such as stage combat or learning to work with special effects equipment. Depending on what kind of role you've landed, this can be quite intensive. You might be matched with industry professionals to help you be ready for the start of production, such as a dialect coach or a fight director.

Character development

Each actor finds their own way to dive deep into their character to prepare for their performance. You may have made a start on this as part of your audition process, and now you can take it further, especially since you now have access to more of the script.

Look for clues about who your character is as a person. This is not only revealed in your lines but also in the way the other characters relate to your character. The script should reveal to you the arc of their story. How do they change over time, and what do they want most? How are they like you, and how are they different? In what ways can you relate to their experiences? Take another look at the character development resource on my website if you haven't already.

Character Development Template

Appearance goals

Pre-production is a good time to focus on your health and stamina, since filming or stage rehearsals can involve long and strenuous days. Some actors need to meet appearance goals for their role during pre-production, which can involve losing weight, gaining weight or becoming muscular via workouts and training. This needs to be done safely. I explore this further in chapter twenty-nine, 'Body Matters'.

Readying experiences

There may be scenes for which actors need to prepare themselves. This could include spending time around a particular culture of people to understand the context of the film better or training in a particular sport to be more convincing in a role. For my role in *Top of the Lake*, I spent some time at a naturist camp to prepare myself for being nude on camera.

Team bonding

As filming looms closer or theatre rehearsals begin, some directors will ask the cast to get together and do some activities so they can bond and chemistry can start building between them. Most directors understand the importance of healthy dynamics between the actors on stage and on set. If the actors are staying together on location, sometimes directors will ask them to arrive a few days before filming starts so they can spend some time getting to know each other. Acting requires us to pretend we are in relationships with each other, but when there are true existing bonds already in place, the job is so much easier.

Depending on what kind of project or production you've been cast in, pre-production will also be when you begin rehearsals. Ahead, we'll take a deeper dive into the different types of rehearsals actors take part in and how they help actors prepare for the camera to roll or the curtain to rise.

CHAPTER TWENTY-FOUR

Rehearsals

I will never forget the first rehearsal I did for a movie called *Bliss*. I was the only character who spoke with an accent, and it was German English. I was terrified that I would freeze or muck up my lines and accent in front of the other actors, the director and the producer. We began by sitting around a table, reading our lines from the script. I was painfully aware that we were inching closer to my dialogue, and then suddenly, the moment was upon me. I said my lines in my German English accent and totally smashed it. I was so relieved and thrilled with the compliments I got from my fellow cast members.

Table reads

The rehearsal I described above is known as a table read, and it's usually the first rehearsal actors do when starting a project. Treat the table read seriously because the director is getting their first glimpse of how the actors interact with each other and how each actor brings their character to life.

For films, it's most commonly used to sharpen dialogue and work out script kinks. Sometimes, problems in casting are identified during the table read. It can reveal, for example, if an actor is not right for a role or if a role needs reworking. A number of actors, including Marisa Tomei, did table reads for the role of Penny in the series *Big Bang Theory* before Kaley Cuoco was cast.[84]

When it comes to TV pilots, a lot of factors may still be undecided, from plotlines to character development. If the pilot is successful or you are cast in an already running show, there will be table reads for each episode so the production team can hear how the dialogue they've written sounds when spoken and do rewrites as required. If you're on a sitcom that's filmed in front of a live audience, jokes can sometimes be rewritten based on audience reactions.

Theatre shows also do table reads. They are generally one of the first rehearsals the cast does before beginning a more intense rehearsal schedule.

Block rehearsals

Block rehearsals are very different for stage vs filming. For theatre productions, blocking is used to work out how the actors will move around the stage during a scene. A lot of thought goes into this, because if there is a lot of dialogue, it can be boring for the audience to watch people standing around talking to each other. Props and set items like furniture help actors move around the stage and position their bodies in a way that's meaningful.

---

84 Boone, K. (2022, November 1). *Marisa Tomei almost played Penny on 'The Big Bang Theory' and says she had no clue the show would be so 'iconic'*. Business Insider.

Blocking for film and television is still about the actors' movement throughout a scene, but it is considered through the lens of a camera. This is the time to work out the camera angles, camera movements and lighting. Marks are placed on the ground by the lighting team to help actors stay within the frame.

Rehearsing scenes

The requirements and frequency of rehearsals vary depending on the production you're cast in. Let's look at how rehearsals might work in each area when it comes to running lines and rehearsing scenes.

Commercials

If you have been cast in a commercial, then I wouldn't expect there to be any rehearsals before the shoot day. They may get you to do one block rehearsal. When shooting, they might start with a wide shot to capture the entire scene, then shoot from different angles and finish with your close up. Hair and makeup will swoop in between takes to adjust your appearance as required. You may get directions from the director, or it may be the assistant director who you work closely with.

There may be more rehearsal time for a commercial if it is a big-name brand with a big budget. I was once in a commercial for a popular beer product, and our director was the infamous Vincent Ward. He had a particular vision in mind for the kind of energy he wanted out of the scene, but we weren't quite hitting it. All of a sudden, he asked us to jump up, go into the studio next door and start throwing a pretend rugby ball to each other. We were diving and jumping around, catching this imaginary ball, until he told us to stop and quickly ushered us back to the film set. We went straight into another take filled with new energy and delivered exactly what he was looking for. It was a bit crazy at the time (and so much fun; I loved it), but it worked, and I guess that's what matters.

Theatre

The start of rehearsals for theatre was always such an exciting time for me. I loved meeting the cast and beginning to work out how we were going to move around on stage. It was exciting just to be on stage, knowing that you're starting the groundwork. I was keenly aware that what I did at each rehearsal would help me shine on opening night, so I made sure I gave it one thousand percent every time.

For a new production preparing to open on the West End or on Broadway, you can expect rehearsals to be six days a week for six to eight weeks. Shows with greater complexity, such as effects and complicated musical scores, have been known to rehearse for sixteen weeks. Bigger stage productions set up a separate stage for the chorus on which to practise big dance numbers away from the main cast, who are practising their dedicated scenes. Rehearsals will become your life right up until opening night.

Movies and television

Somewhere in between lie movies and television. If you want to rehearse with your scene partner, you can do this while you're waiting for your scene to be filmed, or you might agree to do this together when you are off set. When you come to set, sometimes the actors might stand in a circle with the director and do a quick run-through of their lines while waiting for the set to be ready. This is really important for day players, who may not have been at the table read.

Scenes that are heavy in emotion, have special effects or stunt work may have dedicated rehearsal times, as well as anything with musical numbers or dance routines.

Television shows that air five days a week, like sitcoms or soap operas, are filmed at lightning pace. You'll likely get the chance to do your scene a couple of times, and then filming will move on. Your best take will be used.

Technical rehearsals

There are many technical components to a stage production the audience is never aware of. A spotlight shining on an actor in the right spot, a smoke machine coming on at the right time or even an actor's microphone working at the right volume are invisible but crucial aspects to a performance. Technical rehearsals are meticulous and can run over several days to get the lighting and sound correct.

Dress rehearsals

When opening night is fast approaching, the dress rehearsal(s) is crucial for ironing out any remaining crinkles in the performance. Theatre production costumes are expensive, so actors get very few chances to wear them before opening night. Dress rehearsals let actors experience their movement in their costumes with full makeup. A dress rehearsal also allows actors to practise quick costume changes, which happen in the wings and sometimes must be completed in under a minute. This is also their last chance to practise their lines, choreography and hitting their marks before the big day. There's something so magical about putting your costume on. It allows you to transform as an actor to a greater extent.

Rehearsals are an important part of acting and getting you ready for filming or stage productions. Use the time wisely, work with your cast mates and listen carefully to feedback. Soon enough, it will be your time to shine. You want to sparkle, so take the time to polish your performance.

CHAPTER TWENTY-FIVE

On-Set Experiences

Warning: This chapter covers topics that could be triggering for some readers, including sexual harassment and sexual assault.

hen I was twenty-four, I landed a small role in a movie called *Century*, which featured Charles Dance, Miranda Richardson and Clive Owen. It wasn't my first paid job, but it was the first gig involving me wearing an elaborate costume with full hair and makeup. The film was a period piece that required me to be fitted into a whalebone corset-type dress, which was extremely hard to breathe in. It was a surreal experience to be sitting in makeup with Charles Dance next to me; I was totally star struck. He turned to me and said, 'Ya all right, darlin'?', and I remember giggling and giving a shy response. I felt like I'd made it to the big time. The whole experience was a buzz and a blur of cameras and people everywhere. Like me, you could feel a bit overwhelmed when you first start working on a film set. It's a busy place with a schedule and budget to keep everyone focused and on task.

Your first day on set

There are all sorts of experiences you could have when you join a cast and crew. It really depends on the production you've been cast in and what kind of role you've landed. You'll want to start on the right foot, so here are a few tips to help you prepare:

What to bring

Sets are kept secure, so bring some identification. Other than that, you might want to bring something to keep you occupied. It could be a book to read or some podcasts to listen to, so if there's some downtime, you'll have something to help you pass the time. Don't take anything valuable to set unless you have access to a locked area. There should be food and drink provided, but don't overdo it. You don't want to be going to the toilet frequently or boredom eating to the point where you feel bloated or sick.

Don't change your appearance

Your appearance probably factored into your casting on some level, so the studio will expect you to look like you did at your audition when you arrive on set. This is not the time to give yourself an extreme makeover unless you have been specifically asked to alter your appearance as part of the role (we cover this in chapter twenty-nine, 'Body Matters').

Arrive early

When it comes to film sets, time is money. Ensure you've worked out where you're going as well as your transport and parking plans if you plan to drive. A delay caused by an actor turning up late will not be a great way to start.

Find a production assistant

Production assistants are usually moving around quickly with a headset on. Introduce yourself to them as the talent, and they will usher you to where you need to be, whether that's the green room or hair and makeup.

The 2nd assistant director will sign you in to record your hours. If you've been working offsite, make sure you sign out after you've travelled back to the studio and taken your costume off.

Glossary of On-Set Jobs

Working with a director

Unless you are one of the lead actors, it's unlikely you'll have much to do with the director. They will focus their attention on their stars, and the supporting actors will most likely spend their time with the 2nd assistant director. Despite your close proximity, this is not your big chance to meet and impress the film director. Getting in their face is unlikely to help you in the least.

If you have landed a lead role, listen closely to directions given to you by your director. These are called 'actor notes', and they will be tweaks to your character's emotions and actions during a scene. They are generally given as verbal instructions, such as 'This time, say the line to them like it's the last time you'll ever see them.' Try not to be defensive about the director's notes. They have a vision, and it might not be aligned with how you imagined the scene.

I've worked with many directors, and they all have their own special qualities. I personally find that directors who have acting experience have a greater level of empathy for their actors. I'm not saying that directors need to have acting experience, only that it allows them to relate to our experience. I have found it difficult to work with directors who focus heavily on the technical aspects of a scene. They tend to break your scene down into components, such as your entry point, your lines, your action and your exit, like you're on an assembly line rather than in a creative process. Too much focus on the technical delivery of a scene can result in a lack of care for the actor, who may feel under pressure.

'Corpsing'

This is when an actor succumbs to uncontrollable laughter when trying to do a scene that is serious in nature. Although we're talking about laughing, the situation is anything but funny, hence the term 'corpsing', which refers to the murdering of a scene.

Now, sure, if you're doing a comedy and the gags keep making you laugh, you might get away with bursting into laughter at the wrong point. But even then, the people working on set want to get the scene in the can and move on. There comes a point at which you just have to keep a straight face and get through the scene.

Corpsing is a different beast from cracking up at jokes. This is an attack of laughter during a scene or situation that is not funny at all. The pressure to stop laughing because of the nature of the scene only exacerbates the problem. Note that usually the actor is not laughing at the situation portrayed in the scene. It can arise from nervous tension and the body's need to release it. Trying to suppress the laughter generally makes it worse. The actor needs to be given a little time and space to get through the episode, but productions are usually short on time, making the situation even more stressful.

News Anchors Corpsing

I was once doing a scene on the TV series *Power Rangers* when I experienced an attack of corpsing along with my co-star Milo Cawthorne, who was playing the green power ranger. We were supposed to be discussing the deadly 'gamma flu' that was infecting children in our scene. The dialogue was cheesy and a little over the top, but even still, it wasn't a scene that called for laughter, and yet we couldn't hold it in. I was supposed to be chopping vegetables, and each time the director called 'Cut!' due to another fit of giggles, the vegetables had to be reset. We were costing the production time and money with every take; the crew were less than impressed with us. The assistant director ended up separating us so we could get our wits about us. We got through the scene eventually, but it was certainly an unenviable position to be in.

Generally, if you're laughing during a scene that's not funny, you're probably not fully immersed in your character. That's a good thing to notice, so you can work on it. Instead of trying to stop the laughter, which is likely to make it worse, try to focus on doing something physical. Think specifically about how your character is moving in the scene. That will bring your awareness to your body and away from whatever thoughts might cause you to laugh.

Again, from the top

There will be scenes that a director will shoot non-stop until they get what they're looking for. This is one of the hardest parts (in my experience) of being an actor; saying the same lines again and again while the scene is shot from different angles. You need to keep saying those lines as if it's the first time you've said them, bringing fresh energy to the shoot all day long.

Saying the same lines repeatedly can be difficult, but can you imagine having to change those lines after a full day of shooting? That's what happened to me when I was in a bank commercial. I spent an entire day saying one line over and over. They shot me from every angle, and when it came to shooting me from the front, they informed me that the script had changed and I wasn't saying the line right. No one told me the script had changed even after I'd spent hours saying the line incorrectly. Now I had to start saying it differently, which was extremely hard to do. By the end of the shoot, I was shattered. It was gruelling.

It's important to know that just because commercials are generally no more than three minutes long, that doesn't mean the shoot will be short. Prepare for a long day, because a big-name advertiser is out to make millions of dollars off the back of this commercial, and all thanks to you looking great with your bottle of 'insert product here'. So, as long as you've got the right look and feel for what they want, they'll ask you to say that line until they've got it just right.

Safety

I was on a low-budget reality TV show in 2000. It was filmed in Australia, and they had us doing some very questionable tasks. For example, they wanted us to skinny dip in a river, which I refused to do because there could have been crocodiles in the water. I also encountered a poisonous snake in the middle of the night, which was terrifying. I could have been bitten, and the film crew was nowhere in sight. They had all gone to stay at a local hotel some distance away from the actors. They wanted the job done and the money in the bag; they didn't seem to care about our welfare.

Most countries have some form of health and safety governing body that oversees the treatment of employees in workplaces. Some countries have specific regulations for film and television sets, while others only have recommended guidelines in place. America, for example, has OSHA (Occupational Safety and Health Act); however, the legislation has no specific regulations for film and television sets, so they are subject to the same requirements as any other workplace.[85] Considering that some tasks can be high risk in the film industry, such as stunts and the use of weapons/explosives, it's a shame there aren't more dedicated universal regulations in place. Some actors protect themselves by writing specific health and safety expectations into their contracts. In my opinion, film studios would do well to have a dedicated health and safety officer overseeing high-risk filming situations, but this is still considered a 'nice to have' by some.

---

85 The Occupational Safety and Health Act and OHSA Standards, Centers for Disease Control and Prevention.

Violence

Films portray life, and in life there is violence. It's important that the violence simulated in films is closely supervised and coordinated while also not interfering with an actor's flow. Generally, stunt coordinators do the heavy lifting in dangerous scenes, but when the fighting is up close and personal, it's all you.

Sometimes actors agree to purposefully hit each other to create a more realistic scene. If you're thinking about doing this, consider your co-star carefully. An actor is supposed to pull their punches, hitting their co-star with much less force than they actually could, but Sylvester Stallone told his co-star Dolph Lundgren to hit him properly in *Rocky IV*. Perhaps with all the training he'd done for the film, Sylvester thought he could take it, but he didn't account for the fact that Dolph was a trained fighter. He hit Sylvester in the chest with full force, as requested, which landed him in hospital with a swollen heart (that hit is still in the movie today).[86] Sure, actors are often willing to make sacrifices for their art, but your sacrifice should never require you to end up in intensive care for four days like it did for Sylvester Stallone.

---

86 The Tonight Show Starring Jimmy Fallon (2016, January 5). *Sylvester Stallone Had a Pro Knock Out Michael B. Jordan* [Video]. YouTube.

Sylvester Stallone Interview

Problems arise when actors don't agree on boundaries for physical acting. In *Man on the Moon*, Jim Carrey was re-enacting Andy Kaufman's infamous wrestling match with Jerry Lawler. To elicit real anger from the wrestler, Jim spat in his face, and the resulting reaction from Jerry saw Jim taking a trip to the hospital.[87]

Jerry Lawler Interview

Thankfully, I have not been on the receiving end of any on-screen violence, but I was in a commercial where I had to slap an actor take after take. I tried not to hit him too hard, but the director wanted it to be more authentic. He told me, 'I'm going

87 Youtube Wrestling (2015, November 21). *Jerry Lawler tells Steve Austin a great Jim Carrey story Part 2* [Video]. YouTube.

to get your co-star to say something to you. You won't know what he's going to say until he says it, and you're not going to like it.' Well, I can tell you I didn't like it, and I promptly smacked him one. Once I heard 'Cut!' I rushed over to him to see if he was okay. He was also eager to ensure I knew the words that came out of his mouth were not his own.

Child safety

Particular care needs to be taken when working with children on set regarding violent or horror scenes. Children are usually only aware of their scenes and not the plot of the movie. They are usually filmed separately from any scary counterparts. These protections are much harder to put in place for stage productions, where children may have no choice but to be exposed to a scene that could include the portrayal of domestic violence or worse.

Animal safety

There was a time that I was on set during a violent scene that included a couple of dogs. I wanted to rush over and protect them because it was such an intense scene, but thankfully, precautions were in place to ensure the safety of the animals. Unfortunately, not all productions are as concerned about animal welfare. Animal protection charities around the world are continuously advocating for better treatment of animals on film and television sets.[88]

---

88 Animals in Movies and on Television: Cruelty Behind the Scenes, PeTA

Stunts and other high-risk scenes

This is an area of the film industry under greater scrutiny of late. I believe the industry is becoming more safety conscious, but it wasn't always that way. Look on Wikipedia for their 'List of film and television accidents'.[89] It goes back as far as the early 1900s and is a grisly read indeed.

There have been some horrific stories of stuntmen and women who have been seriously injured or killed on set, with studios being sued for damages. Even still, some actors choose to do their own stunts, which is risky. Tom Cruise, for example, did his own stunts for the movie *Mission Impossible – Fall Out*, during which he broke his ankle, halting production for six weeks.[90]

Tom Cruise Interview

Nudity and sex scenes

For a long time, the movie industry approached nude or sex scenes like any other scene without recognition of the sensitive nature of this work. Greater care is now taken (in most cases) with closed sets and intimacy

---

89 List of film and television accidents. (last edited 2023, 20 November) In *Wikipedia*
90 The Graham Norton Show (2018, January 27). *Tom Cruise Reacts to Slow-Mo Footage of How He Broke His Ankle | The Graham Norton Show* [Video]. YouTube.

coaches onsite to ensure actors are comfortable and not left feeling vulnerable. The role of an intimacy coach is to create safe environments and essentially choreograph these scenes, a bit like a dance routine. Katherine Heigl shared in an interview with SiriusXM her appreciation for intimacy coaches when she starred in the series *Firefly*. 'We had an intimacy coach on set for that really difficult and complicated scene with the young Tully, and I just felt such a sense of relief that she was being taken care of, that somebody was there just to simply make sure she felt comfortable, safe and protected.'[91]

Intimacy Coaches

A lot is being asked of the actor in these situations. They have to literally strip themselves bare and deliver a convincing portrayal of intimacy that most of us reserve for our partners. Being naked, being touched, being intimate are all experiences that many, many people struggle with in everyday life. There can be insecurities and personal experiences in terms of sexual assault that make these kinds of scenes all the more challenging.

When I was in my twenties, I was working on a set, and the director needed a couple of stand-ins for a sex scene for lighting. Without hesitation, he called out to me and another bloke to get on the bed and

---

91 SiriusXM (2021, February 3). *Katherine Heigl on Filming Sex Scenes With A Female Director for 'Firefly Lane' | Sirius XM* [Video]. YouTube.

position ourselves for the sex scene. We were fully clothed, of course, but as a survivor of sexual assault, I was anxious about what I was being asked to do, but the director was asking, so I just did it. I'm thankful things have changed since then.

Furthermore, some actors have to navigate feelings of internal conflict during intimate scenes if they are in committed relationships. Even though the onscreen intimacy is simulated, it still requires a level of authenticity that can be difficult for actors who are attached. I've felt those feelings of guilt when I had to kiss a co-star repeatedly while my boyfriend was at home. Worse still, my co-star mistook my acting for real interest and promptly tried to cuddle and kiss me when we were off set. If that was me today, I would have kicked off, but I was young and insecure; I pushed him away playfully with a shy giggle

Film productions have realised, possibly more slowly than they should, that they need to show more sensitivity on set regarding sex scenes. Sharon Stone shared in her memoir *The Beauty of Living Twice* that it was suggested she have sex with her co-star to allow for better onscreen chemistry.[92] She refused, as she should. If a big star like Sharon Stone has been pressured to do something like that, you can only imagine the sorts of things young and unknown actors may be asked to do.

Now that intimacy coaches are used more widely within the industry, no one has to be pressured into having real-life sex with their co-star to create authentic chemistry. The rise of sex scene coordinators allows scenes to be facilitated instead of leaving actors to work out what's appropriate. Strict boundaries and protocols are put in place so every touch is mutually agreed upon.

---

92 Stone, S (2021). *The Beauty of Living Twice* (pp 214-215)

Rape scenes

Even greater care is required when depicting a rape scene. Despite their controversy, rape scenes still feature regularly in television shows and movies. It's true that they can be an important part of a plotline or used to make societal commentary, but it's crucial that directors film these scenes without glorifying sexual violence. A rape scene should not be filmed like a sex scene or play into power fantasy turn-ons. It's crucial that directors think about the young people who may watch these movies and the influence it may have on their perspective of sex. The overused scenario of a man pushing himself onto a woman until she submits herself to him is as old as movies themselves. As more women start to direct rape scenes, we see a new perspective emerging. When women direct these scenes, there is less focus on the physical act itself and instead more is revealed of the trauma happening emotionally to the victim. You can see this in the rape scene of Hannah Baker in *12 Reasons Why*, which was written by Elizabeth Benjamin and directed by Jessica Yu. The act is implied more than it is shown, with priority given to depicting the harm via close-ups of Hannah's face.[93]

If anything, the on-set experiences outlined in this chapter demonstrate how important it is for actors to look after their wellbeing. Through their work, actors are telling stories connected to real-life experiences and emotions. This can mean going to dark places internally and pushing their bodies to the extreme. To that end, I have written an Encore section for this book that explores the importance of actor wellbeing, mindset and how to take care of yourself as you explore the different techniques to connect and disconnect from your characters.

---

93 Highfill, S. (2017, May 14). *13 Reasons Why star, creator on the importance of a woman directing Hannah's sexual assault.* Entertainment Weekly.

ENCORE

CHAPTER TWENTY-SIX

Actor Wellbeing

Acting can be a constant cycle of hope and disappointment. Those with a motivated mindset and a good work ethic generally find the road less treacherous. I personally start off each day telling myself, 'Today is going to be a great day', before I even get out of bed. I do it no matter how I'm feeling, because it gives me a little push to get up and keep going. Starting each day with positivity is important to me, and although there were certainly days when I could wallow, I make it my mission to tell myself each morning that this day will be great. That's what works for me, and I'm sure you'll find a morning ritual that works for you. As an actor, you need to be your own hype guy to keep imposter syndrome at bay. That's not to say you need to be arrogant or egotistical, but a healthy daily dose of courage and confidence will keep you moving forward.

Self-belief

In my experience, building a strong relationship with yourself starts with addressing fears, negative self-talk and unhealthy habits and replacing them with affirming beliefs and self-care. There isn't a magic list of activities or techniques that work for all people, but here are a few common ideas:

- Listening to or saying aloud affirming beliefs
- Positive mirror talk or positive statements on your mirror
- Sleep hypnosis recordings of self-care suggestions
- Counselling or therapy groups that help you dismantle unhelpful thoughts and beliefs about yourself
- Browsing self-development books that encourage a positive mindset

These activities can be helpful on those days when you're feeling a little bit down. Those are the days where your ability to pep talk yourself into putting one foot in front of the other can really help.

But there are times in life where no amount of positive talk will help, and that's okay. I'm not suggesting you slap on a smile when you are going through something truly difficult; toxic positivity has no place here. I've been through life events that made it hard to get out of bed, and at those times, I have given myself grace and patience. To this day, I can go through bouts of depression that seem to come out of nowhere. I have also endured the grief of losing a dear friend and the breakdown of relationships; it's so hard. If you find yourself in a downward mental health spiral, please seek medical advice and get the support you need. Take care of yourself, please.

Work ethic

An actor needs to be willing to work hard, sometimes for little return, to progress in this industry. There are many demands made of actors to fulfil their roles, and though you need to know where your boundaries are, a willingness to learn and/or go through temporary changes to meet the requirements of a role may be required. Here are some questions to consider:

Do you really want this role?

I'll help you out here: the answer is yes. Take every chance you get. When I hear about actors turning down roles because they don't think it's right for them, I think 'You're an idiot'. If you're an actor, then act. I remember getting that pep talk from my agent. He told me there was an audition for a fast-food chain commercial, and at first, I said, 'I don't want to do that'. I thought it would probably be tacky, and I wanted to audition for roles with more substance. My agent said, 'Do you want to be an actor or not?' He was right. If you're an actor, go to your auditions and don't mess around.

I honestly don't care what the role is; if I'm cast, I'll take it. I mean, I've always said I'd love to play a badass b#tch with a gun, and it's okay to have a dream role, but honestly, I would do any role that came my way. You can't hold out for a particular role because whether that role is available is beyond your control. Your choices depend on what's being shot or what plays are coming to town. You might gravitate to a type of acting, such as theatre or films, but I'd caution you against ruling out other opportunities. It's good to get a breadth of experience and have your fingers in lots of different pies.

So, if you get the role, take the role. A long list of actors kick themselves daily for turning down roles for films that ended up being iconic. For example, here is a list of actors that turned down the role of Neo in the movie *The Matrix*:

Will Smith

Nicolas Cage

Brad Pitt

Val Kilmer

Leonardo DiCaprio

Sandra Bullock[94]

It's true! They attempted to make Neo's character female and cast Sandra Bullock, but she turned it down, and so Neo remained a male character and eventually went to Keanu Reeves.

One reason these stars turned down the role of Neo was the lack of experience the Wachowski siblings had in directing big feature films. No actor wants to be remembered for starring in a terrible film. One day, when you're an established actor, you might need to decide if you will take a chance on a project or not, but meanwhile, take the roles and see where they take you.

Are you willing to train in a special skill?

Again, the answer is yes if you truly want to succeed as an actor. We've already covered in chapter ten that you may need to learn special skills for a role, such as combat fighting or horse riding, but there are roles that may require an even greater level of training. This is when your awesome work ethic kicks in. Actors dedicated to their craft and intent on delivering an authentic performance will dive into learning whatever skills are required for the role. It might be a challenging experience, like Channing

---

94 Stowe, D. (2021, February 6). *The Matrix: Every Actor Who Turned Down Neo.* Screenrant.

Tatum learning to tap dance for the movie *Hail Caesar!*[95] Or it may be a fun experience like Daniel Radcliffe taking accordion lessons from 'Weird Al' Yankovic for the movie *Weird.*[96]

Channing Tatum Interview

Daniel Radcliffe Interview

Personal relationships

Relationships can be tricky. When we build strong connections with others, we thrive. When we are in conflict with others, we suffer. No one has perfect relationships all the time, and some people are difficult

---

95 Entertainment Tonight (2016, June 2)). *EXCLUSIVE: Watch Channing Tatum Learn to Tap Dance for 'Hail Caesar!'* [Video]. YouTube.
96 The Hollywood Reporter (2022, September 10). *Daniel Radcliffe on Taking Accordion Lessons From Weird Al: "That's a Real Life Moment"* | *TIFF* 2022 [Video]. YouTube.

no matter what we do. Your ability to build and maintain healthy relationships could be crucial when you are in need of support.

Family and friends

The ups and downs of acting life will be much easier to endure if you have a supportive circle of family and friends. However, it's possible the people in your inner circle may find it difficult to understand your career choice. For anyone standing on the outside looking in, it sure can seem a little crazy to pour so much energy and time into learning a craft that holds no guarantees to a job. After a while, dealing with the confused faces of family and friends may push you to build a new support network of people who understand the drive you have to be an actor and encourage you at every step.

If you already have a supportive network of friends and family, then that's great; nurture those connections and keep them close. It's important to have a safe haven where you can just be yourself. It's also very important to keep people in your life who knew you before you started filming and who will continue to be in your life after you've finished. These are the people who love you for who you are, and they will reel you back in if things get crazy. They'll keep you grounded and centred.

Romantic relationships

Trying to maintain a romantic relationship with someone outside of the industry can be challenging. Sometimes it's easier to date someone who understands the demands of the work, which is why actors often choose to date other actors. Also, when you're in a long-running series or a movie trilogy, you will spend almost every day and minute with the same group of people. It's only natural that some of them will be attracted to each other. Some actors decide to put their love life on hold completely while they focus entirely on their role, which makes a support network of friends all the more important.

Professional relationships

If you're shooting away from home, you'll end up hanging out with the cast and crew all the time. You become like a family. Seeing them every day becomes your life, until one day, before you're ready to realise it, it's all over. All movies, theatre shows and TV series come to an end eventually, and having to say goodbye to it all can be incredibly sad. Director Jane Campion understood this well. She scheduled a funeral scene on the last day of shooting *Top of the Lake*, and we all cried with honest grief that the season was over.

There is some solace in the ongoing relationships and friendships you sometimes take away with you from those projects. Other times, there is a double hit of grief when the people you saw every day and connected deeply with move on and out of touch. Such is life.

Conflict in the workplace

Conflicts are often a result of miscommunication, so learning how to communicate effectively will help you to avoid relationship breakdowns. That means expressing yourself clearly and actively listening too.

I've never worked with another actor who I haven't liked (thank goodness!). Unfortunately, I have had to work professionally with all sorts of people, from producers to executives, who were extremely unpleasant.

When I first came to New Zealand, I was hired by a British producer to work as a runner on a movie set. I had experience as a production manager in the UK, but I had to start from the bottom when I got to New Zealand. That was tough in itself, but it was made all the more difficult by a small group of film crew who were angry that the producer had hired me fresh off a plane instead of one of their friends. The fact that my dad is a Kiwi and I had a New Zealand passport were beside the point; in their minds, I didn't belong. No one deserves to be treated as less than for any reason. It was hard to drag myself to the set every day when people looked at me with daggers in their eyes, but I did it just the same.

It doesn't matter what job or profession you're in, you will come across people you don't like and people who don't like you. So, if you find yourself having to push through a challenging work relationship, my advice to you is to act. You're an actor, so use those skills to get through your interactions. After all, you're never stuck in your professional setting as an actor. Almost all of your work will be for a set time period. Keep your eye on the end of the tunnel and remain civil.

If the negative interactions you're having with cast or crew are becoming a chronic problem (instead of a now-and-then issue), you will need to decide for yourself what you are willing to tolerate and what crosses a line. Being harassed or bullied on a daily basis is not something you should have to endure. I suggest you start by talking it through with your agent before you find yourself overwhelmed and in danger of blowing up on the job. Even if the person you're working with is just begging to be put in their place, gossip spreads, and it could be you who ends up with a bad reputation, even if you were the one being treated unfairly.

Mental health

I love being an actor; it's the best gig in the world, but it is also incredibly tough. Each actor, no matter how well they prepare, will encounter challenges and find themselves under pressure, because it's the nature of the work.

For the longest time, actors have struggled to voice any complaints or concerns about treatment out of fear of being replaced. But, in my opinion, this line of thinking is changing, especially as more and more high-profile people begin to talk openly about their mental health struggles.

It's important that actors look after their emotional, physical and mental health because a lot is asked of them on any given day. Actors can go very deep into their roles and be extremely vulnerable. There can be action shots that require them to be precise. They must hit all their marks so the camera can capture them at the right angles, while also remembering to authentically deliver dialogue. They repeat themselves all day long, and sometimes they burst into laughter or fly into a fit of rage because they just can't do it anymore.

In my opinion, not enough thought has been given to the mental and emotional strain some acting roles put on actors (which we cover in the chapter ahead). From what I can tell, conversations about the importance of mental health have really come to the forefront only since about 2016. Most recently, it's been a topic of interest in the sporting field, where high-profile sports people have refused to participate in competitions to prioritise their mental health.[97]

There wouldn't be many actors who could pull out of projects or halt productions for mental health reasons. There is a genuine fear of being seen as 'difficult' on set, which has led to some actors being written out

---

97 Meister, A. (2021, September 24). *Athletes Are Shifting the Narrative Around Mental Health at Work*. Harvard Business Review.

of storylines or killed off in a TV series. Even big-name actors have been removed from movie projects due to 'creative differences'. In an interview with Looper, Alex Wolff, who played Peter in the movie *Hereditary*, shared the difficulty he had in speaking out about the toll the movie was taking on him: 'This, emotionally, was one of those tough ones. It was one of those ones that really did some gymnastics on my emotional wellbeing.'[98]

Thankfully, discussions about mental health are filtering into the artistic world, and more actors are opening up about their mental health struggles. There can be real anguish experienced by some actors when they tap into real and deep emotions to perform, but I'd like to think we are moving on from the 'tortured artist' suffering for their art. When portraying intense emotions, a strong awareness of who you are is crucial, as it helps to maintain a boundary between yourself and your character. This is more important than many actors realise, and we'll look at this next in acting techniques/methods.

---

98 Lammers, T. (2021, July 27). *Alex Wolff Reveals Why He Was Never The Same After Filming Hereditary - Exclusive.*

CHAPTER TWENTY-SEVEN

Acting Techniques/Methods

A s someone who has always flown by the seat of her pants, I like to do everything and learn everything. I've taken loads of classes over the years covering all sorts of acting approaches and techniques, and I'm still looking to learn more. There's nothing wrong, of course, with training in a particular technique. I did Meisner myself, but I didn't stop there, and I've now ended up with an eclectic mix of methods in my acting toolkit. I've also worked with actors who have studied all sorts of techniques, so I've been able to learn from them. Each acting technique seeks to help you embody the thoughts and feelings of a separate persona. You are essentially living as two people while you act, and this sometimes needs to be navigated carefully. Below, I cover some of the more well-known acting techniques and what to be mindful of when using them.

Stanislavski's method

Konstantin Stanislavski developed an actor training technique that has many components. There are lots of books on it at your local library that will explain it all in full. I'll just be covering the three most commonly referred to elements.[99]

Given circumstances

> This is when you as an actor would take the time to write down as many facts about your character as you can determine from the script. It's an exhaustive process that will help you understand your character right down to the tiniest detail. From here, the actor can start to build the character's profile by asking a series of questions to determine who they are, what their relationships are like and what their objectives are.

The 'Magic If'

> The 'Magic If' requires an actor to put themselves in their character's shoes directly and ask themselves personally how they would act/react if they were in the same circumstance. For example, if your character comes home to find their house has been burgled, you don't have to pretend to be that person, you can imagine 'what if I came home and found my house had been burgled?' No doubt, you'd react in very similar ways. Now you're no longer pretending to be the character, you're just being you and reacting as you would on discovering the robbery.

Emotional memory

> This method uses the tool of accessing your real memories to tap into authentic and deep emotions. Effectively, Stanislavski would

---

99 Gillet, J (2014) *Acting Stanislavski: A practical guide to Stanislavski's approach and legacy*. Bloomsbury Publishing.

encourage actors to focus on a true lifetime event that happened to the actor to evoke emotions and use them as required in a scene.

Using real memories is an effective method to elicit real emotions, but I caution actors to be careful about the memories they choose to repurpose. Memories of unresolved painful experiences may be effective but could linger in your mind and cause ongoing anxiety or even trigger depression. It really does depend on the actor. Some people have processed their trauma, so they aren't so severely affected by reaching back into their past experiences. Yale professor Susan Nolen-Hoeksema published research on the effects of ruminating on negative events, and the results showed that doing so consistently predicted the onset of depression, especially in women.[100] So, again, accessing and remembering past negative events over and over could be harming you in ways you don't even realise. These kinds of techniques do require you to have a level of self-awareness regarding what you can handle and ensuring you have support around you if required.[101]

Katherine Heigl Interview

---

100 Nolen-Hoeksema, S., Wisco, B. E., & Lyubomirsky, S. (2008). Rethinking Rumination. *Perspectives on Psychological Science*, *3*(5), 400–424. https://doi.org/10.1111/j.1745-6924.2008.00088.x
101 Variety (2023, June 7). *Katherine Heigl talks about Denny dying on Grey's* [Video]. YouTube.

The Meisner technique

I have personally trained in the Meisner technique, which teaches actors to respond instinctively to their scene partners through the use of emotional preparation, repetition and imagination.[102] Let's look at these more closely:

Emotional preparation

Sanford Meisner encouraged actors to do something before starting a scene that would trigger the emotional state of the character. It could be recalling a personal memory like Stanislavski suggests, but it could also be something imagined or any tool that evokes the required emotion. If you are unsure about using personal memories, you could think of a movie scene that made you emotional or listen to some music. I was working on a movie where one of the lead actors would sit in her trailer and listen to really sad music before coming on set. You weren't allowed to talk to her when she arrived. She had taken herself to a place, and she needed to remain there until she'd shot the scene. Importantly, Meisner encouraged actors only to use something to prepare the emotion, then when acting the scene, continue instinctively from interactions with their scene partners. In fact, Meisner felt that actors should not predetermine their acting choices and rather improvise their reactions as a scene unfolds.

Repetition exercises

These are done as a sort of back-and-forth dialogue between actors, who repeat and respond to dialogue as it bounces

---

102 Moseley, N (2013) *Meisner in Practice*. Nick Hern Books.

between them. It reveals just how many different ways a line can be delivered and encourages the actor to be present and reactive to their scene partner. It's hard to explain, but have a look online for Meisner repetition exercises and you'll soon see what I mean.

Imagination

The Meisner technique encourages actors to use their limitless imagination to connect with their character rather than relying on the more limited realm of their real-life personal experiences. This has come in handy for me when I've been developing a backstory for a character. I have quite a strong connection with my imagination, and so by the time I'm on stage or in front of a camera, I have dreamed up a whole world for my character with every detail contributing to their personality.

Mind the rabbit hole

The imagination is a powerful tool, but it too, needs to be used with care. Actor Bob Hoskins is well known for his role as Eddie in the live-action animated movie *Who Framed Roger Rabbit?* In 1988, when the film was made, there were no green screens or digital effects. To practise getting his eyeline correct when interacting with cartoon characters, Bob trained his mind to imagine his fictional cast. The problem was that Bob turned on a tap by hallucinating that he struggled to turn off after the film had wrapped. He shared this experience in an interview with Terry Wogan on the BBC in 1989: 'I was loopy, I was totally loopy at the end of it. I learned to hallucinate for eight months very intensely, and I lost control of it.'[103]

---

103 BBC Archive (2022, May 14). *1989: BOB HOSKINS on stardom and ROGER RABBIT | Wogan | Classic Interviews | BBC Archive* [Video]. YouTube.

Bob Hoskin's Interview

Lee Strasberg's method / method acting

Lee Strasberg is known as the father of method acting. Like Stanislavski, there are many books written on him and his methods, below are the most commonly referred to aspects.[104]

Relaxation

Strasberg found that actors who felt stressed and tense were often unconvincing in their performance. To connect with their character and focus fully on their role, actors benefited from relaxation exercises that helped them to be present and free from tension.

Sense memory and affective memory

Affective memory is essentially the same as Stanislavski's emotional memory technique. Actors are encouraged to access a real-life memory to connect with the emotions of the event and allow those emotions to surface as they act out a scene. By introducing 'sense memory', Lee Strasberg invited actors to go

---

104 *WHAT IS METHOD ACTING?* The Lee Strasberg Theatre and Film Institute.

further into the memory, recalling not only the emotions of the situation but sounds, tastes, touch and visualisations to bring about a more vibrant recall and a greater emotional connection.

Method acting myths

David Lee Strasberg is the son of Lee Strasberg and is also the CEO of the Lee Strasberg Theatre and Film Institute. The institute has a whole section on their website dedicated to debunking the myths around method acting that have deemed it a sometimes dangerous technique to use.[105]

Myth - You need to live the same life as your character

Here is a quote from David Lee Strasberg taken from the Lee Strasberg Theatre and Film Institute website: '*[Actors] want truth in acting so [they] experiment with literal truth... it's not viable in most circumstances, and it comes with a cost.*'

An example of this kind of approach to a role was used by actor Adrien Brody, who decided to leave his family, home and girlfriend behind and isolate himself in Europe to prepare for his role as Wladyslaw in the movie *The Pianist*. His character was a Jewish pianist who found himself displaced, disorientated and alone as he hid from Nazi persecution. Adrien wanted to connect with that sense of loneliness and discomfort. He even went further and used a starvation diet to experience the true desperation that comes from intense hunger. Though we can appreciate his reasons for wanting to experience the reality of his character, David Lee Strasberg insists this is not an expected

---

105 Strasberg, L. *Debunking Method Acting Myths with David Lee Strasberg* (2019, December 16) The Lee Strasberg Theatre and Film Institute.

part of method acting and rather an extension of it that some method actors choose to do. For Adrien, being willing to have an immersive experience delivered an Oscar-winning performance, but he shared that it took a toll on him. On the *Charlie Rose Show*, he said, 'emotionally and psychologically, it was one of the darkest times I've been in. I immersed myself in sadness.'[106]

Adrien Brody Interview

It is possible to have an immersive experience to help you connect to your character that doesn't require you to turn your whole life upside down. A character I played had a port wine stain birthmark on her face, and I wanted to experience living with that facial feature. I tried wearing it to town while remaining in character. It was shocking how rude people were to me. They stared and pointed. I had no idea how cruel people could be. A mother and daughter walked past me, and the daughter actually elbowed her mother in the ribs, saying loudly, 'Oh my god, look at her face!' I was right there! I thought to myself, 'I can bloody hear you. I'm not deaf!' It gave me a real sense of the sort of looks my character would get and allowed me to connect to her self-consciousness. That one trip into town was quite enough for me.

---

106 Remembrance of Things Past (2020, March 24). *Adrien Brody Interview on 'Pianist'* [Video]. YouTube.

Myth - You need to stay in character all the time

Another myth that David Lee Strasberg addresses is the idea that method actors need to stay in character offstage or off camera. This is not actually a part of the Strasberg method, but as per the last point, some actors do this as part of their approach to method acting. If you want to see the lengths to which some method actors will go, watch *Jim and Andy: The Great Beyond* to get a behind-the-scenes look at Jim Carrey's immersive acting style.

No acting method or technique is considered the best or the one all actors should learn. Each actor will find a technique that suits them on a personal level, and so I encourage you to learn about as many as possible. As this chapter has outlined, acting techniques can focus heavily on the art of becoming someone else and less on coming back to who you are. It's important that actors can safely untangle themselves from their adopted persona. That process is called 'de-roling', and we cover why it's important and how you might do it in the chapter ahead.

CHAPTER TWENTY-EIGHT

De-roling

Some actors are cast in roles that are perfect for them. They don't even need to act; they can just be themselves, like John Malkovich in *Being John Malkovich*. But for the most part, actors are required to portray someone completely different from themselves.

Looking back, none of the roles I've played have been me. But all of my characters have gone through human experiences that I can relate to. That ability to relate is what enables you to give an authentic performance.

I remember feeling quite overwhelmed when it came to breaking down my character (Prue) in *Top of the Lake*. But I was able to weave together, from my own life, the pieces of Prue that helped me portray her authentically. Prue had been picked on as a child, and her parents were embarrassed by the birthmark on her face. So, even though she was forty, she kept her chin down a lot and sat with shoulders slumped, almost withdrawing into herself. She frowned a lot and was nervous in her mannerisms. There was a physicality to her that I used to bring a greater depth to her portrayal. I'm not Prue, but I certainly know what it feels like to be picked on and feel completely miserable about life. When I tapped into those feelings as they appeared in my life, I felt the separation between us disappear.

What is de-roling?

De-roling is a technique used by actors to consciously remove themselves mentally and physically from the character they are embodying. It is a conscious signal to the brain to shift the state of their mind back to their everyday persona so they can leave any heaviness of their character at the studio or backstage. According to the Australian Actors' Wellbeing Study completed by the University of Sydney in 2015, de-roling is taught in drama schools, but actors seldom remember to use it.[107]

The danger of losing yourself

When I arrived on set for *Top of the Lake*, we were told to spend the day in character. I was eager to do a great job, so I pushed Sarah aside and dived deep into Prue; however, Prue was a hard person to be. She was mistreated and disliked by everyone around her. I reached for those feelings and experiences within me to embody her. Once I got there, I walked around with a heavy weight of self-loathing wrapped around me for the entire day. By the time I got home, I was a mess. I drank heavily and fell into bed feeling depressed.

As important as it was for me to tap into being Prue, it was equally important for me to detach from her. I made a mistake so many actors make. I leapt into Prue without any thought of securing a lifeline back to Sarah. The line between pretending to be a character and actually believing I was the character had become blurred.

---

107 Bailey, S., Dickinson, P. (2022). *The Importance of Safely De-roling.*

A brain imaging study completed by the NeuroArts Lab at McMaster University, Canada, revealed that activity in the part of the brain associated with self-knowledge and self-perception drops off when actors are performing.[108] Actors aren't just forgetting themselves like they might forget to put out the rubbish; the techniques they're using are actually affecting brain chemistry, which is why using them safely is so important.

How to de-role

In my eagerness to get into character, I hadn't thought about how to get back out. There are lots of different ways to de-role, and here are a few you could try:

- Move your body physically and imagine the movement forcing the character out of your body. You could jump up and down and imagine them falling out or kick your legs to fling them out.

- Handing back a specific prop related to the character to the prop master and imagining the character to be within the prop.

- Using a visual reminder, place an object on a table while you are in character and put it away when you are not.

The technique I use was taught to me by fellow actor Robyn Malcolm. She told me that when she wraps at night, she'd remove her costume and then unzip herself from her character like a second invisible costume. To this day, that's one of the best bits of advice I have ever received. I always unzip my character now when it's home time. I physically touch the top

108 Brown, S., Cockett, P., & Yuan, Y. (2019). The neuroscience of *Romeo and Juliet*: An fMRI study of acting. *R. Soc. open sci.*6181908181908 http://doi.org/10.1098/rsos.181908

of my forehead, like I'm grabbing an imaginary zip, and move my hand down my body, pretending that an outer layer of myself is unpeeling. I then step forward like I'm actually stepping out of a full-body cover. As soon as I step forward, I can feel the change in my energy. As I said before, I have a strong imagination and I'm a visual person, so this unzipping technique worked really well for me. When I learned to let go of Prue, I felt like myself again.

There are other things you can do to help shake off your character's persona, story and life experiences. Doing something grounding, like yoga or walking in nature, will help you come back to the here and now. It's also important to connect with friends and family. If you're away from home, shooting on location, maybe a phone call will do. Think of them like an anchor that keeps you connected to who you are.

Drinking to de-role

The traditional de-roling technique on many of the film sets I've spent time on seems to be to head off to a bar for a drink with your fellow cast mates. I'm no party pooper. I love heading out for a drink and getting to know the people I work with after filming. However, there is a danger of becoming dependent on alcohol as a relaxant, and it is more likely to suppress your character than help you detach from them.

The Australian Actors' Wellbeing Study mentioned previously concluded that 43% of males and 36% of females surveyed admitted using alcohol at levels that placed them at moderate risk of harm or above.[109]

---

109 Szabó M, Maxwell I, Cunningham ML, Seton M. Alcohol Use by Australian Actors and Performing Artists: A Preliminary Examination from the Australian Actors' Wellbeing Study. Med Probl Perform Art. 2020 Jun;35(2):73-80. https://doi.org/10.21091/mppa.2020.2012 PMID: 32479582

I caution actors against using drinks as a regular way to unwind. I've had to walk away from people I cared about because they would not acknowledge their alcohol dependency. That was a very painful experience, but you cannot save someone who does not want to be saved. I know this because I had to save myself from my own substance addiction when I was younger; thankfully, I got the help I needed.

Some roles are stressful on mental, emotional and physical levels. Find your own de-roling technique so the stress you endure does not spread beyond the stage or film set. Characters can have very harsh experiences and trauma as part of their story. That's why it's important to know where you finish and your character begins. This can be made even more challenging if you have to go through a body transformation to portray the character. Seeing your reflection change can mess with your psyche. Furthermore, changing your body is a big commitment to undertake and could have long-lasting effects. We explore the challenge of body matters in the next chapter.

CHAPTER TWENTY-NINE

Body Matters

T he movies I watched growing up generally showed me a singular body type and appearance. Women were slender and attractive; men were tall and strong. Thankfully, we are now living in a world where a greater number of films include a diverse range of body types and appearances, though we still have a way to go. We want to see life on the screen, and life comes in all shapes and sizes.

Even after watching all those movies as a youngster, one of my best roles turned out to be an overweight, disfigured woman; go figure. You don't know what role you might land one day and what it may require from you regarding your body size. There are some unhealthy and potentially dangerous methods for rapid weight change, so it's important to understand the risks and have support as you go through a body transformation.

Gaining weight

Some actors want to have an authentic experience when playing a character who has a larger physique, so they choose to increase their body size. Charlize Theron gained fifty pounds to naturally portray an overwhelmed and exhausted solo mother in the movie *Tully*, but it came at a price. She shared with People TV: 'I ate a lot of processed sugar. It put me into a terrible depression. My soul felt heavy. I was really unhealthy. I threw my back out, I couldn't sleep, I was lethargic.'[110]

Charlize Theron and Weight Gain

Jared Leto also encountered problems when he put on sixty-seven pounds for his role as Mark Chapman in *Chapter 27*. He said in an interview with the *Guardian*: 'Really, it's a stupid thing to do. I got gout, and my cholesterol went up so fast in such a short time that my doctors wanted to put me on Lipitor, which is for much, much older people.'[111]

It's truly no joke what rapid weight gain can do to your body systems. It's not just about putting on some fat; your body must adjust and acclimatise to a new way of functioning, and the effects can be long lasting. There seems to be less support on offer to actors who are gaining weight for a role because they are large rather than muscular. If you decide to go down this route, definitely work with a doctor and nutritionist to find the safest way to do it while causing the least amount of internal harm.

---

110 People (2018, May 4). *Charlize Theron Says Losing 50 Pounds In Her 40s Is A Lot Harder | People TV | [Video]*. YouTube.
111 Patterson, J. (2014, Feb 1). *Jared Leto: 'I road-tested my character to get a little judgement, some meanness, a little condemnation'* The Guardian.

Body suits

Some actors can get around the perils of weight gain by wearing a 'body suit', which is certainly a healthier alternative. That's what actor Chris Sullivan did for his role as Toby in the popular TV series *This is Us*. For the purpose of storytelling, the body suit worked really well as the episodes flicked back in time to when his character was larger and forward to when he was slimmer. However, there was some backlash to the use of the body suit by viewers who felt the role should have gone to an actor who was large, as larger actors are so often overlooked for roles.[112]

Chrissy Metz on Body Suits

Gaining muscle mass

It might seem like becoming muscular would be a healthy thing to do, but that's not necessarily true. The workouts and diets can be extreme, and some actors have shared that they dehydrate themselves before filming to make their muscles appear more pronounced. Henry Cavill of *Superman* fame shared on the *Graham Norton Show*: 'It's the worst part of it. Diet is

---

112 Watch What Happens Live with Andy Cohen (2017, Feb 17). *Chrissy Metz Talks Chris Sullivan's 'This Is Us' Fat Suit | WWHL* [Video]. YouTube.

difficult, and you're hungry, but when you're dehydrated for three days, you get to the point on the last day where you can smell water nearby.'[113]

Henry Cavill on Dehydration

It's a technique commonly used by bodybuilders and needs to be closely monitored. Those who try to go it alone are in danger of injuring their bodies or harming their internal organs.

Will Poulter of Guardians of the Galaxy fame shared with the Independent his concerns about the extreme diet and exercise regime he went through with Marvel: 'Your physical and mental health has to be number one, otherwise you end up promoting something that is unhealthy and unrealistic.'[114]

Channing Tatum shared similar sentiments on the *Kelly Clarkson Show*, saying that he could not imagine how people who work a nine-to-five job could stay in shape since working out was a full-time job for him to keep his 'Magic Mike' physique.[115]

---

113 The Graham Norton Show (2023, July 1). *The VERY Best of Henry Cavill | The Witcher | The Graham Norton Show* [Video]. YouTube.
114 Harrison, E. (2022, April 9). *Will Poulter: 'Method acting shouldn't be used as an excuse for inappropriate behaviour – and it definitely has'* The Independent.
115 The Kelly Clarkson (2022, February 17). *Channing Tatum Is Struggling To Get In Shape For 'Magic Mike 3'* [Video]. YouTube.

Channing Tatum Interview

If you land a role that requires you to build a muscular physique, I suggest your agent includes a clause in your contract that adequate support from professionals in nutrition and fitness will be provided. If that can't be arranged, then you could try to find your own support crew to help you stay motivated and keep you safe.

Losing weight

Rapid weight loss can also be damaging to your health, especially if you are trying to achieve an emaciated and/or underweight physique. Reducing the amount of food you eat also means reducing your nutrient and vitamin intake. This needs to be considered carefully as you go.

Much has been made of Matthew McConaughey's forty-seven-pound weight loss for his role in the movie *Dallas Buyers Club*. Fortunately, Matthew sought advice on how to drop the weight as safely as possible. He shared on the *Ellen Show*: 'I met with nutritionists first to work out how to safely lose three pounds a week over four months.'[116]

---

116 The ElleDeGeners (2013, November 6). *Matthew McConaughey on Losing Weight on Ellen show* [Video]. YouTube.

Matthew McConaughey Interview

Jared Leto (who I mentioned before) was also cast in *Dallas Buyers Club* as a transgender person, and like Matthew, lost a significant amount of weight. Their dedication to their roles is admirable, but there are some Hollywood commentators concerned that actors like Matthew and Jared have set a standard of expectation in the acting industry. Actors may find themselves pressured to take unhealthy risks to be considered dedicated enough for a role.[117] I've made it clear that dedication and a strong work ethic are required to be a working actor, but equally important is a firm understanding of what your boundaries are and what you are willing or not willing to do for your art.

Jennifer Lawrence, for example, was under pressure to lose weight for her role as Katniss in the movie *The Hunger Games* because her character was supposed to be malnourished. But she pushed back, instead wanting to portray the character as strong and healthy. She shared in an interview with BBC *Newsnight*: 'We have the ability to control this image that young girls are going to see. It's an amazing opportunity to rid ourselves of the unrealistic expectations of this industry.'[118]

---

117 Lim, P. (2013, November 12). *Actors Losing Weight For Roles is Not Glamorous, It's Dangerous* MIC.
118 BBC Newsnight (2013, November 12). *Jennifer Lawrence talks body image – BBC Newsnight* [Video]. YouTube.

Jennifer Lawrence Interview

No matter what kind of body transformation you're asked to do, the important thing is that you do it safely. Hopefully, the studio will provide support from professionals, but if that's not on offer, you will need to decide for yourself if this is something you can do and whether you have enough support to make it happen.

Plus-size actors and stereotypes

This is me, but I refer to myself as being of 'the larger human variety'. The roles I am offered to audition for are very specific. There are few roles for actors with larger body types where their weight is not a central part of their story arc. We are living lives, have families, careers and all sorts of experiences, but put us in a film and we have nothing going on for us except being large.

Plus-size actors like Amber Riley who starred as Mercedes on the TV show *Glee* found weight loss pressure from the industry incredibly hard. She was being offered roles for characters that she described as 'sitting in the corner, loathing themselves'. In an interview on MTV's *This is how I made it*, she shared: 'I never wanted to play a character that hated herself. I wanted people to know that those aren't the only kind of roles for people like me.'[119]

---

119 Stack, T. (2012, November 16). *'Glee' Star Amber Riley gets real on MTV's 'This Is How I Made It'* Entertainment Weekly.

In my view, slender, white, cis-het people can be cast in almost any role. As soon as an actor is outside of that definition, they are in danger of being typecast. People of colour, plus-sized people, people with disabilities or actors from the LGBTQ+ community may have their characters written with a fixation on their perceived difference. The 'fat funny person', for example, has pigeon-holed people with larger body types into roles that commonly use self-deprecating humour. In an interview with the *Guardian*, Rebel Wilson shared that her decision to lose weight for health reasons received pushback from her management team: 'They asked me why, why would I do that? Because I was earning millions of dollars being the funny fat girl'.[120]

Rebel Wilson Interview

There are many other tired and worn-out body stereotypes, from the skinny nerd to the stupid, muscular jock and the pretty, mean girl.

> Actors can bulk up, lose weight, gain weight or adorn a body suit to meet appearance requirements, but it would be good to see greater care being taken in approaches to body changes and a little outside-the-box thinking in regards to casting. They say art imitates life, but I think screenplays and casting have a little work to do to show the

---

120 BBC News (2021, December 7). *Rebel Wilson on weight loss, health and fertility* [Video]. YouTube.

true complexity of humanity. Perhaps we'll see more variety in story narratives when we see more diversity in the writers having their works produced. Male writers have been dominating the space for a long time, but change is afoot.

CHAPTER THIRTY

Women in the Industry

I loved watching old black-and-white movies when I was little. I wanted nothing more than to be a Ziegfeld Follies girl, gliding around on stage in a feathered gown. The starlets were gorgeous, the men handsome, and for reasons lost on me as a child, all the bad guys seemed to be Russian or German. When I pursued my dream of being on stage, I learned the path to being a female actor is not paved with rhinestones and feathers as I'd imagined. I've experienced first-hand the difficulties of being a woman in the industry, and those challenges remain today. The industry has changed in some ways, but there's still much to do to create a fair and accurate representation of women in roles and to provide equal opportunities for their success.

A bit of history

The origins of theatre have been linked to the times of ancient Greece, thousands of years ago. Many of the earliest Greek tragedies and comedies involved female characters from goddesses to wives and daughters, but they were always played by men. The reasons why pertain to a general perception during these times that women were inferior. Women were restricted in their movement, clothing and activities, and they certainly were not allowed to make a spectacle of themselves on stage. Despite this being the case thousands of years ago, this position held firm right up to and including the days of Shakespeare, when women's roles continued to be played by males. Women only appeared on stage as recently as the 1600s, and even then it was a slow and gradual change, starting with operas.[121]

It's amazing to me that even in today's world you can still come across negative comments about female singers or actors who are 'making a spectacle of themselves'. This is literally an ancient point of view, and I find it so exhausting that its echo remains. Women are spectacular; they deserve to be spectacles just as men have been for millennia.

Women weren't alone in their struggles to take the stage. Just as men would dress as women to portray female characters, white men would wear blackface to portray people of colour, who also found themselves shut out of the spotlight. The use of blackface was offensive enough, but it grew worse with the rise to 'the minstrel shows' common in America in the late 1800s. These shows used vulgar and racist comedy to depict African Americans and their culture with stereotypical characters.[122]

Even when films took the plunge to cast black actors, such as Hattie McDaniel (who was the first black female to win an Oscar for her role in *Gone with the Wind* in 1940), the roles remained stereotypical. A look at Hattie's filmography on Wikipedia will show you a long list of roles she played as a maid, cook or servant. Her Oscar achievement is,

---

121 Women's Museum of California (2017, September 6). *Get thee to a Stage! A Brief History of Women in the Theater* Women's Museum of California.
122 Clark, A. (2023, March 29). *How the History of Blackface is Rooted in Racism* HISTORY

unfortunately, overshadowed by the terrible treatment she received at the ceremony, which was held at a 'whites only' hotel. She was made to sit at a small table on the edge of the room while her other nominated white cast members, Vivien Leigh and Clark Gable, sat at another table with director Selznick.[123]

The casting couch

When the door opened for women to begin auditioning for acting roles, it wasn't without a price, and by that I am referring to the establishment of the 'casting couch'. This term refers to occasions where actors are expected to do sexual acts to be cast in a production. Though its exact origin is hard to pinpoint, tales of a casting couch have been linked to the Broadway theatres that opened in the early 1900s, predating Hollywood studios.[124]

However it started, what's important is that the casting couch is seen for what it is: an abuse of power. The focus should not be on whether an actor gave sexual favours in exchange for being cast in a role, but that they were asked or expected to do so. It is the unbalanced power dynamic between hopeful actors and top-level executives that allowed the casting couch to exist at all.

It concerns me that some hopeful young actors may mistakenly believe that the casting couch is a normal part of show business. I've said in the previous chapter that you need to have the right attitude and work ethic to excel as an actor, but that doesn't mean you should be willing to lose your dignity or a piece of your soul. Do not fall into the trap of thinking you should do whatever it takes to get a role. Who you choose to sleep

123 Hattie McDaniel (last edited 2023, 23 November) In *Wikipedia*
124 Zimmer, B. (2017, October 16). *'Casting Couch': The Origins of a Pernicious Hollywood Cliché* The Atlantic.

with is your own business, but increasing your chances of being cast in a role should not factor into that decision (in my opinion). If you're a woman who wants to make it as an actor, then let it be your acting talent that gets you there. There is no reason for casting and sexual acts to be mixed together, and if anyone tells you otherwise, run.

I was so disappointed to realise halfway through dinner with a potential employer that he was expecting sexual favours in exchange for a job. I was disgusted and a little bit panicked about how to get out of that situation. I really wanted that job, but I had to walk away from it. After that, I made sure I always paid half at dinner or even paid for the lot to ensure there would be no misunderstandings or assumptions that I owed anyone anything.

#metoo

The #metoo movement gained global recognition and momentum in 2017. The misuse of power was well known in the industry but not talked about or confronted until women started speaking up and shaking up how things are done. As a result, a lot of people have become more aware of how they conduct themselves in workplaces and whether their behaviour is appropriate.

It's had a ripple effect in many ways. I'm sure we've all had to stop and think about the jokes we tell and the conversations we have in professional environments. If this movement has helped even me to consider how I conduct myself, then you can bet there'll be some big names at the top who have quickly started behaving themselves.

As a survivor of sexual assault, I am only too happy to see the tides turn with the #metoo movement. It's time for women to be treated fairly and acknowledged as the intelligent and capable people they are. A friend of mine told me she's been teaching her son that 'no means no, and don't try to convince me'. I think that's a great statement because it's about respecting a woman's voice. In professional settings, for example, I've noticed that some people think my decisions are illogical and I just need a bit of convincing. They've ignored my stance and pushed against me until I ended up going against my gut and saying 'yes' when I originally said 'no'.

Staying true to yourself and trusting your intuition is so important. Decide for yourself what goes against your moral compass and stick to it. Talk to your agent about anything that feels wrong, and remember you have every right to walk away from unhealthy situations.

Female character development

When you consider how long it took for women to even step foot on a stage, you can see why we are still struggling to change how female characters are portrayed in movies. Here are a few ways we continue to see room for improvement:

Women writers

> Male writers continue to have their works made into plays, television shows and films at a greater rate than females. The San Diego State University Centre for the Study of Women in Television and Film completed a report that stated of the top 250 grossing films in the United States completed in 2022, 19% had women writers.[125]

> In general, women writers are having a tough time getting

125 Lauzen, M. M. (2023) *The Celluloid Ceiling: Employment of Behind-the-Scenes Women on Top Grossing U.S. Films in 2022*

their scripts made into productions. This may come from an assumption that stories written by females are niche in their content. That women would only write romantic comedies or fluff pieces. You only need to watch a series like *The Handmaid's Tale* to see that women-orientated stories are not doomed to be about kittens and butterflies.

Tropes

With fewer women's work making it to production, female characters keep falling into tropes, such as the damsel in distress or the manic pixie girl. These characters are written for the development of the male protagonist, and they aren't trusted to carry the plot of the story. The struggle for female characters to be written with depth is shared by members of the LGBTQ+ community. The same queer characters turn up in scripts over and over again in roles such as the 'gay best friend' or the 'hyper-sexualised queer'.[126] The LGTBQ+ community has asked again and again for better representation. There are signs of change occurring; for example, the TV series *Sex Education*, which has been celebrated for its well-written queer characters.

The Bechdel Test

Used by cartoonist Alison Bechdel in the 1980s, Alison drew a comic of a conversation where two queer women agreed they wouldn't go and see a movie unless it met three criteria:

1. It had at least two female characters in it
2. They spoke to each other

---

126 Medina, H. (2021, June 15). *Top 10 Overdone LGBTQ Tropes* What's Trending

3. About something other than a man[127]

This test became a mainstream method for measuring female representation since around 2010. You would be surprised how many popular films fail this test. Here are a few:

Avatar (written by James Cameron)

The Avengers (screenplay by Joss Whedon)

The Edge of Tomorrow (screenplay by Christopher McQuarrie, Jez Butterworth, John-Henry Butterworth)

The Girl with the Dragon Tattoo (screenplay by Steven Zaillian)[128]

The test offers a very low bar for measuring the depth of female characters and yet so many fail. The greatest determining factor of whether or not a film passes this test is the presence of a female writer on the team. Here are some that passed:

Hidden Figures (screenplay by Alison Schroeder and Theodore Melfi)

Girl, Interrupted (screenplay by Lisa Loomer, Anna Hamilton Phelan and James Mangold)

Bridesmaids (written by Annie Mumolo and Kristen Wiig)

---

127 Bechdel, A. (2005, August 16) *The Rule* Alison Bechdel.
128 Heffernan, R. Lyons, J. (2023, August 21) *From 'Oppenheimer' to 'Avatar': 13 Modern Movies That Surprisingly Fail the Bechdel Test.* Collider.

The Devil Wears Prada (screenplay by Aline Brosh McKenna) [129]

The Bechdel Test has limitations, and since its creation, more sophisticated tests have been created to measure the lack of depth in female characters in fictional works. Measuring this lack is one thing, but doing something to address it is another.

Female directors

The movie industry has been male dominated for so long, many females with writing or directing aspirations wind up in assistant roles. Even roles like grips or operating the cameras are usually seen as jobs for men. There just seems to be a general lack of confidence in women's abilities to be in leading positions, both in front of or behind the camera.

Where big budgets are concerned, there still seems to be a lingering notion that women directors cannot create big blockbuster hits. Obviously, no one told that to Patty Jenkins, who was given a two hundred million USD budget to create *Wonder Woman* (2017), which grossed over eight hundred million USD worldwide.[130] Men and women both have to earn a reputation for creating good movies before they can get a chance at a big-budget movie. The problem is that it's taking women longer to get enough movies under their belt to step into the realm of possibility. Niki Caro's first big-budget movie was *Mulan* in 2020; however, she had been directing films for thirty years before she was given that chance.[131] I

129 Deen, B. (2021, December 13) *The Best Movies That Pass the Bechdel Test.* The Women's Network.
130 Wonder Woman (2017 film), In *Wikipedia*
131 Erbland, K. (2017, March 29). *'The Zookeeper's Wife' Director Niki Caro Has a Plan for Fighting Hollywood's Gender Gap.* IndieWire.

think the industry would see a lot of positive growth and change if more women were given the chance to be in roles previously dominated by men. I'm not talking about women taking over the industry; I'm talking about equal opportunities for women at all levels. There's room at the table for everyone.

For the longest time, women were believed to be weak and less intelligent than men. A story about a strong woman who takes care of herself would have been considered unrealistic in the 1950s. But it was a reality for so many women, including my mum. She was born in 1936 and worked in many unconventional sectors, such as farming, carpentry and on trains. She wasn't the least bit interested in just being a pretty girl (though she truly was stunning). She had bigger muscles than most of the men in our small village, and she wouldn't allow anyone to disrespect her. She was a pioneer in many ways; a feminist leading the way for the women of today.

She's the sort of woman girls need to see in films. They need to see the full range of vocations and adventures that real women experience and not some dreamed-up ideal. I was fortunate to have a role model like my mother, who was a total go-getter. She might have been considered strange, but she didn't wait to be whisked away by a prince, she fought hard to do things her way. I guess it rubbed off on me in some ways, because I didn't suffer fools when I entered the workforce and I still don't. I put up with more than I should have, though. I'd get tapped on the butt and treated like a coffee b#tch. I knew I could do so much more than what was being asked of me, but I was told I had to stay in my lane. So, I got out of that lane; I didn't stay where I wasn't growing. I lasted fifteen minutes working at a 'hot potato' eatery because my boss insisted that I needed to be shown how to spread butter. Perhaps the people I worked with had also grown up watching *Cinderella*-type movies and had mistakenly come to believe that women are incompetent. That they don't know how to think for themselves and need to be told what to do.

We have progressed now with movies like *Frozen*. The main character isn't rescued by a man, and she reclaims her own power. That story moved me to tears, because we do need to dissolve this idea drummed into girls that you will be rescued and looked after by someone else. The truth is life is bloody hard, and the only person who will get you where you want to go is you.

THAT'S A WRAP

I hope that what I've shared with you over the last thirty chapters has given you some valuable insights into acting as a career and all the possibilities it holds. I'll leave you here with some final reflections based on my experience and knowledge.

You will make mistakes

As a young person, I thought it was terrible to make mistakes. I avoided making them or being caught making them as much as possible. The truth is, it's impossible to live a human life without making mistakes, and in fact, it is through mistakes we learn our most valuable lessons. It's a painful realisation for us all. We are going to make mistakes as much as we loathe them, and the best we can do is own them and learn from them.

Trust your intuition

Sometimes those mistakes happen because you didn't trust your instincts. Learn to listen to your gut. In a production, leading actors get lots of direction and smaller parts are sometimes left to work things out for themselves. This is where your intuition will serve you. There have been times where I've felt a little unsure about what the director wanted me to do, but I just tapped into those instincts, and most of the time they've been spot on. So, trust your abilities, and if you're completely lost and think you're in danger of mucking up the scene, check with someone if you can.

Take it day by day

Sometimes I've been cast in a role, and I've thought to myself, 'I've finally made it!' I assumed this role would bring me the next one and that one would bring me the next one and so on and so forth. I'd gotten ahead of myself, and although it's okay to be hopeful, it's also important to remember anything can happen and things don't always go the way you think they will. Work comes and it goes. You may find yourself pushed into the spotlight and pushed out again. In my case, a glimmer of hope appeared that I might see my star shoot. But I learned, as many do, that you really have no control over the direction of your star. Celebrities star in movies that flop and unknowns become famous unexpectedly overnight. The best thing you can do is work hard at whatever roles come your way and see where they take you.

Forget fame

I caution actors against aiming for fame. Being famous is not fun and games at all. I've been a personal assistant to famous people, and although it may look glamorous, it truly is a very hard existence. I like to visualise a lead role or Oscar-winning performance in my future, but I'm also mindful of staying in the here and now. Because when you start thinking that your happiness hinges on getting a particular role or winning a particular award, you'll be constantly reaching for that and never be happy with where you are or what you've got. It's okay to strive for more, but when you make that the focus of your life, you miss the real and important things right in front of you.

Acting truly is the best thing in the world, in my opinion. It's true that it can be difficult to get regular work, but I would never call the actors who do 'lucky'. Almost all of them have worked their butts off to get into that situation, and I can almost guarantee there was no luck involved. Just because we see them once they're finally on screen or on stage doesn't mean it wasn't a long, hard road for them to get there. So, take the stars out of your eyes, and just concentrate on being the best actor you can be. Little more can be asked of you.

So that's it! It's the end of my book. Go out there and smash it. I hope you're able to put some of what I've shared into action and that it helps you progress in your acting journey. Go be your best self and I look forward to seeing you on the silver screen.

Q & A WITH HOLLY HUNTER

I had the absolute pleasure of interviewing Holly Hunter about her acting journey as an added bonus for this book. I really enjoyed our rich conversation and I hope you also enjoy what she so generously shared with me.

Q: What was your first paid acting gig, and what did it teach you?

I went to a conservatory training school for four years at Carnegie Mellon University in Pittsburgh, Pennsylvania. After graduation, I immediately flew to New York. Three weeks after landing, I got this job as a glorified extra in a horror movie. I met all these actors in midtown Manhattan, and we got on a bus that took us to a location six hours away. We stayed there for six weeks as a community of actors. They weren't people I had graduated with, I didn't know any of them, but it was like an instant family. With the right group, it can feel that way. There can be an instant familiarity or even an intimacy with other actors, because that's kind of what we do for a living. But it does need to be with the right group. So that's what happened for me in 1980, and it was enormously valuable to hit the ground running in New York city with that sense of family.

Q: What are your tricks for memorising lines?

I don't really have a trick, but I love to memorise lines with someone else. I know that there are all these apps that are available where you can memorise lines on your phone alone but I really love to have somebody with me. Preferably, I like them to be with me in the room, but if I can't have the person in the room with me, I'd have them on Zoom. I need that connection with somebody, because at the end of the day, it's a human interaction; you're in scenes with people. So, I need to be in scenes with people from the beginning. That's what I prefer. It brings me into a performance space.

Q. You have a degree in drama. What is the most valuable thing they taught you at university?

That there's something sacred to be protected about acting and about bringing a story to life. That it's precious. Yes, it can be fun, but it has intrinsic value, and an actor can take that very personally. You hold onto that. You protect that as an actor.

Q. What are your best tips for approaching and delivering a great audition process?

I would never say that what I share is advice; it's simply my experience, because the way that I do things may not work for other people. Actors sometimes do things antithetically to me, the complete opposite, and they're brilliant and amazing; I look in awe at what they do.

Audition-wise, I would have my agent call them and say, 'Holly would like to come into the room and read. She wants to go straight into the scene, and then after she's finished, she would like to meet everybody and talk.' My feeling is always to protect the scene and protect myself. So, I walk into the room with the intention of the scene.

There isn't a character that wouldn't feel nervous about something, so I incorporate my own sense of being afraid into the scene. Even if the character is pretending to not be scared, that has been helpful to me to work in. Sometimes I've walked into a room and I've wanted it to be a different way. Once, I asked someone if I could use their chair as a way of making the space mine and claiming my audition. I didn't ask in a hostile way or in an aggressive way, just in a confident way.

Q. Do you still have to audition anymore?

After I got an Oscar, I auditioned for a movie called *Living Out Loud*. They didn't see me in the role, and I said, 'Please, let me audition', and I got that role. More recently, I have not auditioned because people can look back and see my stuff. I might meet the director or the producers. If it was something that they didn't see me being able to do but I saw me in the part, I would be happy to audition.

Q. What's your advice for dealing with rejection?

People take rejection so differently. Actors just take so much rejection. Even if it's not rejection specifically, actors have to live with unemployment. We have to live with not working. I'm not acting twelve months of the year; if I was, then I'd be working too much. I'd start feeling like I'm depleting my reservoir. I love to work, and I love not working. In terms of rejection, you've just got to take it, feel it, and you have to take it on. I have a tendency just to move through it.

Q. When you take on a role, how do you build your character?

It depends on what the role is. If I'm going to be a cop, I'll go hang out with some cops. If the character is good at certain things, I'll go and get instruction from someone who can help me with that. Any activity that my character is really good at doing, I want to study that activity. I want to at least get a rudimentary comfort level with it. Sometimes I will go to an Alexander teacher (which is a particular kind of movement vocal work) to help me approach a character. That can be really private and special work.

One of the things I always do is I break a script down and do a script analysis. Sometimes I do it by myself, or I do it with someone else, like an acting coach. I love to break a script down scene by scene. I'll go through and write down any time my character talks about herself and any time my character is mentioned by other people. I'll make note of what my character says about other people. Who talks about who and what? That's kind of fun to see how that breaks down. I go through every scene and think, okay, what does my character want in this scene? What is my character doing to other people to get what she wants? What are the obstacles preventing her from getting what she wants?

Q. Do you ever get nervous on set? If you do, how do you calm yourself?

Frequently, I deal with nerves, I always have. It's enlivening, and I think a certain level of nerves can help with creativity, which is born from a certain level of stress. Creativity can also be born out of incredible amounts of relaxation. I don't reject the stress of being nervous or being afraid. Like I said before, maybe your character is afraid too? Incorporate that fear into the scene. I've got to negotiate with my fear so that it doesn't overwhelm me. I will do relaxation exercises before a scene. If I'm too nervous, I will go and be with my scene partners if that helps. It's all very intuitive. But I deal with it, I don't ignore it. I don't pretend that it's not happening. If I'm nervous, I'm acknowledging it.

Q. In what ways do you think the #metoo movement has changed the movie industry?

It's helped so much. I'm seeing many more female directors; we're moving forward at a much faster rate. Jane Campion had a female director of photography (DoP). I've actually been working with lots of female DoPs and female directors. Men have to understand that the old playing field is not going to happen anymore and there's going to be consequences. There are a lot of ways women have been shamed to go underground with this stuff. Now there are ways to deal with this in public and out in the open. It's such a relief.

Q. What would you like to see change for women in the industry?

I would love to see more scripts written by women, because women have a point of view that can be radically different. We need come into contact with those stories; we need to hear much more of that voice. People say, 'oh those are chick flicks', as though it's a pejorative that they are less than. I think those days have got to be over. I don't like the simplistic ways in which women's stories have been dealt with. I'd like to see their complexity brought more to the fore.

Q. How do you feel after a shoot has wrapped?

It depends on how much I loved that character and the experience. When we did *Top of the Lake*, we all had such a great time doing it, it was a bummer when it ended. It was hard to say goodbye to everybody and to Jane. I allow myself to feel depressed afterwards and try to be easy on myself for a couple of weeks. I'm generally quite exhausted from a shoot because they have intensity.

Q. Do you find comedic roles easier or harder than others?

It's really fun to go to work and laugh. It's just so much fun, and I love to laugh with the other actors. I love to see what people are going to do. If they're shooting a scene, I love to walk to the set and hear their voices. Doing a comedy is really fun, and right now I'd say I prefer doing comedy, because that's what I've been around and I find it so delightful.

Q. What makes a good director, in your opinion?

Each director is completely different. The directors that I've enjoyed working with have taken care of me. That's the one characteristic they all had in common; I felt taken care of. I didn't feel intimidated, obliterated, dissed or invisible. If I feel any of those things, I don't consider them a good director. If I have to take care of a director, that's another bad one. I don't want to take care of the director; I want the director to take care of me. I wouldn't call a director a parent, but there is something parental about taking care of a set, and that is a director's responsibility.

Q. Have you ever had to work with someone you didn't like? Like a co-star? And if you had to be on set with them every day, how did you deal with it?

I've worked with actors who worked really differently from me, but by and large, I tend to love my fellow actors; I just do. Even if there is a difference of opinion, there is almost always something about an actor that I'm working with that I respect. There's almost always something about them that I hold in a high regard. They might have a particular intelligence about the script, for example. I would ask them, 'What do you think could be better with this scene?' Because there may be something that's breaking down in the writing, or perhaps there's a blocking issue. I try to hone in on what I value about this person.

Q. Have you ever worked with an accent coach? What accents do you know?

I like to play with my voice. Right now, the character I'm doing has a vocal pitch that is quite lower. It's fun. I spent several months doing a play where I was playing someone from Ireland; I felt a certain kinship with that dialect. I had a good handle on the Scottish dialect when I did the bookends for *The Piano*. A British dialect, I think, would be very challenging, I've never tried it. I think it's particularly challenging for

Americans to do a great British accent. The accent coach that I worked with used phonetics because I'd learned phonetics at college. That's a great fundamental guideline that puts us on the same page and gives us a language that we can use.

Q. What did you enjoy most about being on Broadway?

Broadway is kind of a legendary thing. There's a real sparkle about being on Broadway just geographically. I love that part of New York; I love those blocks that make up Broadway. I love the theatres. They're a little big to me. I wish the house was smaller so it could be a slightly more intimate experience. I love walking in the stage door. I love doing stage. I love the immediate relationship with the audience.

Q. What is your advice for actors who are trying to get the attention of an agent?

Everything is so different now. I've had the same agent for years. Now social media is the way people get themselves out there. Some agents need for people to be extremely active on social media, they need them to have a lot of followers in order to get a job. That's kind of wild.

Q. With the pressure of fame, what keeps you grounded?

I live my life as if I'm not famous. I'm an actor, and I'm not that famous. My fame is not an impediment to me. Sure, it can help me get a restaurant booking or theatre bookings, I like that. Other than that, I kind of ignore it. People can make a lot of room for their own fame if they really love it; I tend to leave it alone.

BIBLIOGRAPHY

Chapter Two

MsMojo (2018, November 27). *Top 10 Actors You Didn't Know Got Their Start on YouTube* [Video]. YouTube. https://www.youtube.com/watch?v=V4vWe6lqcUk

Chapter Three

OxfordUnion. (2016, October 26). *Oliver and James Phelps | Full Q&A | Oxford Union* [Video]. YouTube. https://www.youtube.com/watch?v=ey0o69yYSFs&t=138s

Child, B. (2014, July 7). *Star Wars Episode 7 adds two more cast from open auditions.* The Guardian. https://www.theguardian.com/film/2014/jul/07/star-wars-episode-7-add-two-more-cast-from-open-auditions

WatchMojo. (2014, February14). Top 10 Celebrity Commercials from Before They Were Stars [Video]. YouTube. https://www.youtube.com/watch?v=g7Nuwo0LLGk

Chapter Five

Gilliss, G. (2021, May 13). Be the New Triple Threat: Actor-Writer-Producer. *Backstage.* https://www.backstage.com/magazine/article/new-triple-threat-actor-writer-producer-51268/

Rosie O'Donnell. (2022, September 8). *Matt Damon Interview – ROD Show, Season 2 Episode 63, 1997* [Video]. YouTube. https://www.youtube.com/watch?v=1vKbNyRnAMQ&t=148s

NZ On Screen. (2023, April 3). *Taika Waititi.* https://www.nzonscreen.com/profile/taika-waititi/biography

Taika Waititi. Credits. IMDb, https://www.imdb.com/name/nm0169806/fullcredits

Lindbergh, B. (2019, Feb 7). *The Rise of the iPhone* Auteur. The Ringer. https://www.theringer.com/movies/2019/2/7/18214924/steven-soderbergh-high-flying-bird-iphone-tangerine-unsane-netflix

Kevin Smith. (2015, December 28). *22 years ago, I sent this incomplete budget along with a copy of #Clerks to @miramax in hopes they'd buy my flick.* [Image attached] [Status update]. Facebook. https://www.facebook.com/YesThatKevinSmith/photos/a.77596326929/10153159633456930/

Sundance Film Festival 2022 At-A-Glance. Film submissions. Sundance, https://www.sundance.org/wp-content/uploads/2022/01/SFF2022-At-A-Glance-internal-update-with-late-add.pdf

Chapter Six

ABC News. (2013, February 2). *Hollywood's Favorite Extra in GoDaddy Super Bowl Ad* [Video]. YouTube. https://www.youtube.com/watch?v=xYGXHknKdVY

WhatCulture. (2021, September 26). *10 Huge Actors You Didn't Notice As Extras in Movies* [Video]. YouTube. https://www.youtube.com/watch?v=o2pv_2HxA10

Chapter Seven

HitFix. (2013, December 19). *Steve Carell and Paul Rudd discuss hilarious improv moments for 'Anchorman 2'* [Video]. YouTube. https://www.youtube.com/watch?v=bx1wBxyAmnM

Fox 29 Philadelphia. (2023, July 18). *Comedian and actress Tig Notaro on the legendary 'Hello, Good Evening, I Have Cancer' standup set* [Video]. YouTube. https://www.youtube.com/watch?v=GdzCAFX946c

Danica Patrick. (2021, Nov 9). *Daniel Whitney | Larry the Cable Guy | Comedy Gave me Confidence | Clips 01 |* [Video]. YouTube. https://www.youtube.com/watch?v=5OZl3CzquHs

Brown, M. (2015, March 27). *Why Tina Fey is a Screenwriting Trailblazer.* The Script Lab. https://thescriptlab.com/features/screenwriting-101/3239-why-tina-fey-is-a-screenwriting-trailblazer/

Vitale Perez, M. (2022, November 5). *Stand-Up Comedians Who Became Great Actors.* Movieweb. https://movieweb.com/stand-up-comedians-great-actors/

Chapter Eight

Brown, S. (2018, August 15). *15 Actors You Didn't Know Had Musical Theater Backgrounds.* Backstage. https://www.backstage.com/magazine/article/actors-know-musical-theater-backgrounds-13646/

Diseases & Conditions. *The gut-brain connection* (2023, July 18). Harvard Health Publishing. https://www.health.harvard.edu/diseases-and-conditions/the-gut-brain-connection

Chapter Nine

Oliver, D. (2015, April 14). *The Vaesline Camera Trick That Gave Old*

Hollywood Actresses A Gorgeous Glow. HuffPost. https://www.huffpost.com/entry/vaseline-camera-trick-effect_n_7062900

Wolf, D. (2012, February/March). *Jack Foley and the Art of Sound.* Irish America. https://www.irishamerica.com/2012/01/jack-foley-and-the-art-of-sound/

Evangelista, R. (2023, August 26). *This is the First Movie to Ever Have a Twist Ending.* Collider. https://collider.com/first-movie-twist-ending/

Ferguson, M. (2021, October 3). *How the Blair Witch Project Changed Movie Marketing.* Screenrant. https://screenrant.com/blair-witch-project-trailer-marketing-viral-campaign-influence/

Wiki. Websites. Lostpedia Fandom, https://lostpedia.fandom.com/wiki/Websites

Oceanic Airlines, TV Tropes https://tvtropes.org/pmwiki/pmwiki.php/Main/OceanicAirlines

Jurassic Park, Industrial Light & Magic. https://www.ilm.com/vfx/jurassic-park/

OSSA Movies. (2022, January 5). *Die Hard Without Stunts and Effects | OSSA Movies* [Video]. YouTube. https://www.youtube.com/watch?v=wQ2cJP2Yynw

The A.V. Club. (2021, December 1). *Kirsten Dunst and Jesse Plemons Interview: The Power of the Dog* [Video]. YouTube. https://www.youtube.com/watch?v=HYAcErenkKQ&t=23s

Joseph Campbell (1949) The Hero With a Thousand Faces. Princeton NJ: Princeton University Press.

Christopher Booker (2004) The Seven Basic Plots: Why We Tell Stories. London: Continuum.

Chapter Ten
Gagnon, R., & Nicoladis, E. (2021). Musicians show greater cross-modal integration, intermodal integration, and specialization in working memory than non-musicians. Psychology of Music, 49(4), 718-734. https://doi.org/10.1177/0305735619896088

60 Minutes. (2014, November 17). *Sword Fighting stories from "The Princess Bride"* [Video]. YouTube. https://www.youtube.com/watch?v=mvFcfZ2LBJQ

Vudu. (2018, April 5) *I, Tonya Behind the Scenes – Creating the VFX (2018) | Movieclips Extras* [Video]. YouTube. https://www.youtube.com/watch?v=bYpMLomQt-U

SearchlightPictures. (2011, Feb 15) *BLACK SWAN, Featurette: Natalie Portman's Training.* [Video]. YouTube. https://www.youtube.com/watch?v=_ekWWP0dQZM

Chapter Eleven
Understanding Your Learning Style (2008) Wilfrid Laurier University.

Ose Askvik Eva, van der Weel F. R. (Ruud), van der Meer Audrey L. H. The Importance of Cursive Handwriting Over Typewriting for Learning in the Classroom: A High-Density EEG Study of 12-Year-Old Children and Young Adults. *Frontiers in Psychology* 11, (2020). https://doi.org/10.3389/fpsyg.2020.01810

Ludke, K.M., Ferreira, F. & Overy, K. Singing can facilitate foreign language learning. *Mem Cogn* 42, 41–52 (2014). https://doi.org/10.3758/s13421-013-0342-5

Potkin KT, Bunney WE Jr (2012) Sleep Improves Memory: The Effect of Sleep on Long Term Memory in Early Adolescence. PLoS ONE 7(8): e42191. https://doi.org/10.1371/journal.pone.0042191

Chapter Twelve

Movieclips. (2011, May 28). *Jaws (1975) – The Indianapolis Speech Scene (7/10) | Movieclips* [Video]. YouTube. https://www.youtube.com/watch?v=u9S41Kplsbs

Davidson, L. (2023, May 9). *The Deadly Sinking of the USS Indianapolis.* History Hit. https://www.historyhit.com/sinking-of-the-indianapolis/

Movieclips. (2012, March 16). *Morning Routine – American Psycho (1/12) Movie CLIP (2000) HD* [Video]. YouTube. https://www.youtube.com/watch?v=RjKNbfA64EE

Movieclips. (2012, May 22). *The Red Dress – Requiem for a Dream (6/12) Movie CLIP (2000) HD* [Video]. YouTube. https://www.youtube.com/watch?v=oYcKftzUS_Y

Child of the 80s. (2018, September 2). *1989 – Steel Magnolias – M'Lynn's Breakdown (Sally Field)* [Video]. YouTube. https://www.youtube.com/watch?v=HTOzFKNGtpc

Movieclips. (2014, January 15). *Taxi Driver (5/8) Movie CLIP – You Talkin' to Me? (1976) HD* [Video]. YouTube. https://www.youtube.com/watch?v=-QWL-FwX4t4

Chapter Thirteen

Warner Bros. Entertainment (2014, May 23). *Alexander: The Ultimate Cut | Theatrical 10th Anniversary – Behave | Warner Bros. Entertainment* [Video]. YouTube. https://www.youtube.com/watch?v=aKJjAwrtLOU

Schaefer, S. (2022, March 23). *Filming Crouching Tiger, Hidden Dragon Was A Constant Struggle Behind The Scenes.* Slashfilm. https://www.slashfilm.com/807853/filming-crouching-tiger-hidden-dragon-was-a-constant-struggle-behind-the-scenes/

Miller, A. (2019, May 15). *Jodie Comer reveals how she became the accent queen as Villanelle in Killing Eve, thanks to her father.* Metro. https://metro.co.uk/2019/05/15/jodie-comer-accent-queen-villanelle-killing-eve-season-2-father-9559329/

Carlson, E (2019) *Queen Meryl: The Iconic Roles, Heroic Deeds, and Legendary Life of Meryl Streep.* Hachette Books

Feder, S (Director). (2020) *Disclosure* [Film] Netflix

Melamedoff, M (Director). (2017) *The Problem with Apu* [Film] truTV

Ansari, A, Yang, A, Jarman, Z (Writers). Wareheim, E (Director). (2015, November 6) *Indians on TV* (Episode 4, Season 1 Master of None)

Towers, A. (2021, May 11). *Fisher Stevens regrets doing brownface in Short Circuit: 'It definitely haunts me'.* Entertainment Weekly. https://ew.com/movies/short-circuit-fisher-stevens-regrets-playing-indian-role/

Howard, R (Director). (1992) *Far and Away* [Film] Universal Pictures

Chapter Fourteen
Zoe Bell (2020, May 2). *BOSS BITCH FIGHT CHALLENGE – Zoe Bell* [Video]. YouTube. https://www.youtube.com/watch?v=dCO0DXAc0tk

Chapter Fifteen
All Alumni. Alumni & Industry. NIDA, https://www.nida.edu.au/alumni-and-industry/all-alumni

Prominent A.C.T. Alumni, A.C.T. Alumni, A.C.T. https://www.act-sf.org/training/a-c-t-alumni/

Meet our LAMDA Acting Alumni, Acting Alumni, LAMDA https://www.lamda.ac.uk/students-alumni/acting-alumni

Alums Take home Emmys (October 2015). The Julliard Journal https://journal.juilliard.edu/journal/1509/alums-take-home-emmys

Famous Actors who didn't go to Acting School. IMDb, https://m.imdb.com/list/ls027968240/

Roach, V. (2015, May 5). *Stars that were rejected by drama school.* News.com.au. https://www.news.com.au/entertainment/celebrity-life/stars-that-were-rejected-by-drama-school/news-story/8efbd750fc1ccf63b209b0e699807bad

Vilhauer, J. (2019, December 31). *Why Speilberg, a Film School Reject, Was Successful Anyway.* Psychology Today. https://www.psychologytoday.com/nz/blog/living-forward/201912/why-spielberg-film-school-reject-was-successful-anyway

Chapter Sixteen

Resources. AAANZ, https://aaanz.co.nz/resources/

Chapter Seventeen

Dockterman, E. (2018, July 26). *How Georgia Became the Hollywood of the South: TIME Goes Behind the Scenes.* TIME. https://time.com/longform/hollywood-in-georgia/

Lodderhose, D. (2022, June 23). *Hot Spots: How Manchester Is Fast Becoming A Magnet For International Productions* DEADLINE. https://

deadline.com/2022/06/hot-spot-manchester-magnet-international-productions-1235050010/

Why the World's Biggest Movies and TV Shows are Filmed and Produced in B.C. BCBUSINESS. https://www.bcbusiness.ca/why-the-worlds-biggest-movies-and-tv-shows-are-filmed-and-produced-in-bc

Summerlin, D. (2014). The Walking Dead. In *New Georgia Encyclopedia*. Retrieved June 8, 2017, from https://www.georgiaencyclopedia.org/articles/arts-culture/the-walking-dead/

The Howard Stern Show. (2018, November 13). *Hugh Jackman Recalls His Days Working as a Clown* [Video]. YouTube. https://www.youtube.com/watch?v=dr_KsWizEuA

Finn, N. (2023, June 25). *These Stars' First Jobs Are So Relatable (Well, Almost).ENEWS.* https://www.eonline.com/news/1377689/these-stars-first-jobs-are-so-relatable-well-almost

Chapter Eighteen

GQ. (2017, November 3). *Stranger Things' Dacre Montgomery's Insane 'Billy' Audition Tape | GQ* [Video]. YouTube. https://www.youtube.com/watch?v=cJ1zhq3yNBM

The Project. (2022, June 5). *Austin Butler On How Auditioning In A Bathrobe Made Him A King* [Video]. YouTube. https://www.youtube.com/watch?v=fHyyZIJBecw

Chapter Nineteen

Pichardo, G. (2023, June 27). *What to Know About 4-7-8 Breathing.* WebMD. https://www.webmd.com/balance/what-to-know-4-7-8-breathing

Mink, C. (2021, January 8). *How 'Stranger Things' Got Made.* Backstage. https://www.backstage.com/magazine/article/how-stranger-things-got-made-69464/

Chapter Twenty

The Tonight Show. (2016, March 22). *Jake Gyllenhaal Bombed His Lord of the Rings Audition* [Video]. YouTube. https://www.youtube.com/watch?v=nIVU6W3EDcU

The Howard Stern Show (2019, September 16). *Melissa McCarthy Almost Quit Acting Days Before Landing 'Gilmore Girls' (2014)* [Video]. YouTube. https://www.youtube.com/watch?v=3nEDAnNFcuM

Gennis, S. (2014, June 12). *Shailene Woodley on Being Cut from Amazing Spiderman 2: "Was I Awful?"* TVGuide. https://www.tvguide.com/news/shailene-woodley-amazing-spider-man-2-1082883/

UCD – University College Dublin (2011, November 10). *"I couldn't believe what I saw – I wasn't in it!" Christopher Lee on 'The Return of the King'* [Video]. YouTube. https://www.youtube.com/watch?v=Zg_Vd-kLdDU

Chapter Twenty-One

The Graham Norton Show (2019, November 2). *"What Jennifer Aniston, Reece Witherspoon & Dame Julie Andrews Stole from Sets* [Video]. YouTube. https://www.youtube.com/watch?v=zuVUp2qEnHE

Good Morning America (2017, July 19). *"Did Mark Ruffalo Accidentally Reveal That Everyone Dies In Avengers Infinity War?* [Video]. YouTube. https://www.youtube.com/watch?v=_A0UeT38CLo

Associated Press (2009, May 11). *Bale Apologizes for Angry Rant* [Video].

YouTube. https://www.youtube.com/watch?v=KTo_9FYCE1Y

Chapter Twenty-Two

Open Access Extension/EMC Phase Out Frequently Asked Questions. Actors Equity. https://www.actorsequity.org/join/OA-EMC-FAQ/

Wintour, P. (2020, December 18). *Labour abandons the closed shop – archive, 1989* The Guardian. https://www.theguardian.com/politics/2020/dec/18/labour-abandons-the-closed-shop-archive-1989

"Screen Actors Guild." International Directory of Companies Histories. Retrieved November 15, 2023 from Encyclopedia.com: https://www.encyclopedia.com/books/politics-and-business-magazines/screen-actors-guild

Chapter Twenty-Three

Boone, K. (2022, November 1). *Marisa Tomei almost played Penny on 'The Big Bang Theory' and says she had no clue the show would be so 'iconic'.* Business Insider. https://www.insider.com/marisa-tomei-the-big-bang-theory-almost-played-penny-2022-10

Chapter Twenty-Five

The Occupational Safety and Health Act and OHSA Standards, Centers for Disease Control and Prevention https://www.cdc.gov/niosh/learning/safetyculturehc/module-5/2.html

The Tonight Show Starring Jimmy Fallon (2016, January 5). *Sylvester Stallone Had a Pro Knock Out Michael B. Jordan* [Video]. YouTube. https://www.youtube.com/watch?v=23DkAI9183I

Youtube Wrestling (2015, November 21). *Jerry Lawler tells Steve Austin a great Jim Carrey story Part 2* [Video]. YouTube. https://www.youtube.com/watch?v=JWNAS9h9K1Q

Animals in Movies and on Television: Cruelty Behind the Scenes, PeTA https://www.peta.org/issues/animals-in-entertainment/animals-in-film-tv/

List of film and television accidents. (last edited 2023, 20 November) In *Wikipedia* https://en.m.wikipedia.org/wiki/List_of_film_and_television_accidents

The Graham Norton Show (2018, January 27). *Tom Cruise Reacts to Slow-Mo Footage of How He Broke His Ankle | The Graham Norton Show* [Video]. YouTube. https://www.youtube.com/watch?v=QLFRGj-PPNI

SiriusXM (2021, February 3). *Katherine Heigl on Filming Sex Scenes With A Female Director for 'Firefly Lane' | Sirius XM* [Video]. YouTube. https://www.youtube.com/watch?v=4sTHwrZUFPY

Stone, S (2021). *The Beauty of Living Twice* (pp 214-215)

Highfill, S. (2017, May 14). *13 Reasons Why star, creator on the importance of a woman directing Hannah's sexual assault.* Entertainment Weekly. https://ew.com/tv/2017/05/14/13-reasons-why-hannah-sexual-assault-jessica-yu/

Chapter Twenty-Six

Stowe, D. (2021, February 6). *The Matrix: Every Actor Who Turned Down Neo.* Screenrant. https://screenrant.com/matrix-neo-turned-down-actors/

Entertainment Tonight (2016, June 2)). *EXCLUSIVE: Watch Channing Tatum Learn to Tap Dance for 'Hail Caesar!'* [Video]. YouTube. https://www.youtube.com/watch?v=2G1rI8dcD10

The Hollywood Reporter (2022, September 10). *Daniel Radcliffe on Taking Accordion Lessons From Weird Al: "That's a Real Life Moment" | TIFF* 2022 [Video]. YouTube. https://www.youtube.com/watch?v=jXyue460Bns

Meister, A. (2021, September 24). *Athletes Are Shifting the Narrative Around Mental Health at Work.* Harvard Business Review. https://hbr.org/2021/09/athletes-are-shifting-the-narrative-around-mental-health-at-work

Lammers, T. (2021, July 27). *Alex Wolff Reveals Why He Was Never The Same After Filming Hereditary - Exclusive.* https://www.looper.com/470053/alex-wolff-reveals-why-he-was-never-the-same-after-filming-hereditary-exclusive/

Chapter Twenty-Seven

Gillet, J (2014) *Acting Stanislavski: A practical guide to Stanislavski's approach and legacy.* Bloomsbury Publishing.

Nolen-Hoeksema, S., Wisco, B. E., & Lyubomirsky, S. (2008). Rethinking Rumination. *Perspectives on Psychological Science*, *3*(5), 400–424. https://doi.org/10.1111/j.1745-6924.2008.00088.x

Variety (2023, June 7). *Katherine Heigl talks about Denny dying on Grey's* [Video]. YouTube. https://www.youtube.com/shorts/BnOojH_tivk

Moseley, N (2013) *Meisner in Practice.* Nick Hern Books

BBC Archive (2022, May 14). *1989: BOB HOSKINS on stardom and ROGER RABBIT | Wogan | Classic Interviews | BBC Archive* [Video]. YouTube. https://www.youtube.com/watch?v=FUj8PJ0NeCc

WHAT IS METHOD ACTING? The Lee Strasberg Theatre and Film Institute. https://strasberg.edu/about/what-is-method-acting

Strasberg, L. *Debunking Method Acting Myths with David Lee Strasberg* (2019, December 16) The Lee Strasberg Theatre and Film Institute. https://strasberg.edu/blog/debunking-method-myths-with-david-lee-strasberg/

Remembrance of Things Past (2020, March 24). *Adrien Brody Interview on 'Pianist'* [Video]. YouTube. https://www.youtube.com/watch?v=XZS0mqGzGP8

Chapter Twenty-Eight

Bailey, S., Dickinson, P. (2022). *The Importance of Safely De-roling* https://www.researchgate.net/publication/361379066_The_Importance_of_Safely_De-roling

Brown, S., Cockett, P., & Yuan, Y. (2019). The neuroscience of *Romeo and Juliet*: An fMRI study of acting. *R. Soc. open sci.*6181908181908 http://doi.org/10.1098/rsos.181908

Szabó M, Maxwell I, Cunningham ML, Seton M. Alcohol Use by Australian Actors and Performing Artists: A Preliminary Examination from the Australian Actors' Wellbeing Study. Med Probl Perform Art. 2020 Jun;35(2):73-80. https://doi.org/10.21091/mppa.2020.2012 PMID: 32479582

Chapter Twenty-Nine

People (2018, May 4). *Charlize Theron Says Losing 50 Pounds In Her 40s Is A Lot Harder | People TV |* [Video]. YouTube. https://www.youtube.com/watch?v=rxng4WN93Ek

Patterson, J. (2014, Feb 1). *Jared Leto: 'I road-tested my character to get a little judgement, some meanness, a little condemnation'* The Guardian. https://www.theguardian.com/film/2014/feb/01/jared-leto-dallas-buyers-club

Watch What Happens Live with Andy Cohen (2017, Feb 17). *Chrissy Metz Talks Chris Sullivan's 'This Is Us' Fat Suit | WWHL* [Video]. YouTube. https://www.youtube.com/watch?v=-uacOvppDlo

The Graham Norton Show (2023, July 1). *The VERY Best of Henry Cavill |*

The Witcher | The Graham Norton Show [Video]. YouTube. https://www.youtube.com/watch?v=umV4DToYRik&t=10s

Harrison, E. (2022, April 9). *Will Poulter: 'Method acting shouldn't be used as an excuse for inappropriate behaviour – and it definitely has'* The Independent. https://www.independent.co.uk/arts-entertainment/tv/features/will-poulter-guardians-of-the-galaxy-dopesick-b2047322.html

The Kelly Clarkson (2022, February 17). *Channing Tatum Is Struggling To Get In Shape For 'Magic Mike 3'* [Video]. YouTube. https://www.youtube.com/watch?v=pmYFHuaxYdw

The ElleDeGeners (2013, November 6). *Matthew McConaughey on Losing Weight on Ellen show* [Video]. YouTube. https://www.youtube.com/watch?v=oVWO-uyTzgo&t=103s

Lim, P. (2013, November 12). *Actors Losing Weight For Roles is Not Glamorous, It's Dangerous* MIC. https://www.mic.com/articles/72931/actors-losing-weight-for-roles-is-not-glamorous-it-s-dangerous

BBC Newsnight (2013, November 12). *Jennifer Lawrence talks body image – BBC Newsnight* [Video]. YouTube. https://www.youtube.com/watch?v=U3HU7e1XrYA

Stack, T. (2012, November 16). *'Glee' Star Amber Riley gets real on MTV's 'This Is How I Made It'* Entertainment Weekly. https://ew.com/article/2012/11/16/amber-riley-this-is-how-i-made-it-video/

BBC News (2021, December 7). *Rebel Wilson on weight loss, health and fertility* [Video]. YouTube. https://www.youtube.com/watch?v=eyKm2OuD-s0

Chapter Thirty

Women's Museum of California (2017, September 6). *Get thee to a Stage! A Brief History of Women in the Theater* Women's Museum of California https://womensmuseum.wordpress.com/2017/09/06/get-thee-to-a-stage-a-brief-history-of-women-in-the-theater/

Clark, A. (2023, March 29). *How the History of Blackface is Rooted in Racism* HISTORY https://www.history.com/news/blackface-history-racism-origins

Hattie McDaniel (last edited 2023, 23 November) In *Wikipedia* https://en.wikipedia.org/wiki/Hattie_McDaniel

Zimmer, B. (2017, October 16). *'Casting Couch': The Origins of a Pernicious Hollywood Cliché* The Atlantic https://www.theatlantic.com/entertainment/archive/2017/10/casting-couch-the-origins-of-a-pernicious-hollywood-cliche/543000/

Lauzen, M. M. (2023) *The Celluloid Ceiling: Employment of Behind-the-Scenes Women on Top Grossing U.S. Films in 2022* https://womenintvfilm.sdsu.edu/wp-content/uploads/2023/01/2022-celluloid-ceiling-report.pdf

Medina, H. (2021, June 15). *Top 10 Overdone LGBTQ Tropes* What's Trending https://whatstrending.com/10-lgbtq-tropes/

Bechdel, A. (2005, August 16) *The Rule* Alison Bechdel https://dykestowatchoutfor.com/the-rule/

Heffernan, R. Lyons, J. (2023, August 21) *From 'Oppenheimer' to 'Avatar': 13 Modern Movies That Surprisingly Fail the Bechdel Test.* Collider. https://collider.com/modern-movies-bechdel-test-fail

Deen, B. (2021, December 13) *The Best Movies That Pass the Bechdel Test.* The Women's Network. https://www.thewomens.network/blog/the-best-movies-that-pass-the-bechdel-test

Wonder Woman (2017 film), In *Wikipedia* https://en.wikipedia.org/wiki/Wonder_Woman_(2017_film)

Erbland, K. (2017, March 29). *'The Zookeeper's Wife' Director Niki Caro Has a Plan for Fighting Hollywood's Gender Gap.* IndieWire https://www.indiewire.com/features/general/the-zookeepers-wife-director-niki-caro-hollywood-gender-gap-1201797778

Glossary of industry terms

ACKNOWLEDGEMENTS

I am incredibly grateful to everyone who contributed to the creation of *'The Actor's Guide'*. This journey wouldn't have been possible without the support, guidance, and expertise of some exceptional individuals.

My Rock: Charlie

Special recognition goes to my son, Charlie, for enduring and embracing all the ups and downs of having a mum like me. Your patience, kindness, and understanding made this endeavour even more meaningful. I am lucky to have you by my side. Love you to the moon and back xoxo.

Strength and Inspiration: Angela and Peter Valentine

A heartfelt thank you to my mum, Angela, the strongest woman I know. Your resilience, tenacity, and get-up-and-go attitude have made me the person I am today. Your strength has been a guiding light throughout this adventure, and I am endlessly grateful for your love and influence. Thank you also to my brother, Peter, for your unwavering support. Your encouragement has been a source of strength, and I am truly grateful for the presence of both Angela and Peter in my life.

Pillars of Support: Alison, Hazel, Alex, Amy and Charlie

My dear friends, your unwavering support, encouragement, and friendship are like pure gold. You are my gals and I love ya.

In Gratitude to the Stars of "Top of the Lake" and Visionary Director: Jane Campion

A profound thank you. Working on this TV series was the most amazing experience of my life, and I am indebted to you for the opportunity to be a part of your creative world.

An Inspiring Mentor: Holly Hunter

I extend my deepest gratitude to you. Your generosity in sharing insights about your remarkable career and experiences enriched this book. Your time and wisdom have been invaluable, and I am honored to have learned from such a seasoned professional.

Wisdom from the Stars: Robyn Malcolm, Elisabeth Moss, and Sara Wiseman

Heartfelt thanks for graciously offering your invaluable advice. Your wealth of experience and excellence as actresses has left an indelible mark on my understanding of the craft.

Ghost-writer Extraordinaire: Bronwyn Bay

Thank you for your incredible talent and the dedication you poured into ghost writing this book. Your words brought my vision to life, and your collaboration has been instrumental in shaping 'The Actor's Guide'.

This book is a product of the collective efforts and generosity of these remarkable individuals. Thank you all for being a part of my journey in the world of acting and for making 'The Actor's Guide' a reality.